**Editor**
Kim Fields

**Editorial Project Manager**
Mara Ellen Guckian

**Managing Editors**
Ina Massler Levin, M.A.
Karen Goldfluss, M.S. Ed.

**Illustrator**
Alexandra Artigas

**Cover Artist**
Denise Bauer

**Art Production Manager**
Kevin Barnes

**Art Coordinator**
Renée Christine Yates

**Imaging**
Ralph Olmedo, Jr.
Craig Gunnell

**Publisher**
Mary D. Smith, M.S. Ed.

# Year Round Preschool READING

**Authors**

*Brenda Shelton Strickland, M.S. C.A.S.*
*Mary Franklin Green*

Teacher Created Resources

**Teacher Created Resources, Inc.**
6421 Industry Way
Westminster, CA 92683
www.teachercreated.com
**ISBN-1-4206-3185-3**
©2006 Teacher Created Resources, Inc.
Made in U.S.A.

# Table of Contents

# Introduction

Young children develop reading and writing skills in a variety of ways and at different ages. Some are visual learners while others learn best by listening, or through tactile or musical experiences. The activities in *Year Round Preschool Reading* are designed to provide interactive, fun, and effective experiences for preschoolers.

*Year Round Preschool Reading* offers teachers ideas to promote the development of literacy skills for young learners. Topics include the following:

- phonemic awareness

- environmental print

- visual discrimination

- concepts of print

- the alphabet

- phonics

- fine motor skill development

These developmentally appropriate activities will allow children to explore their environment while they build a foundation for learning to read and write.

This book was designed to aid new and veteran teachers, home-based schoolteachers, and independent daycare providers. The cards and activities will provide preschoolers with the hands-on tools they need to help them discover crucial concepts about the English language. Concept assessments and assessment ideas are included with each topic. The literacy overview on page 4 summarizes and defines this book's topics. The page may be enlarged to create a classroom poster or given as a handout to parents.

*Year Round Preschool Reading* offers educators ideas that focus on individual literacy concepts and provides suggestions for individual and group activities. Each activity includes a materials list, step-by-step instructions, and easy-to-assemble reproducible patterns. These hands-on activities offer multiple learning experiences for children at all stages of letter, sound, and word knowledge. The activities are interchangeable to provide variation, enrichment, and remediation in different settings. Nothing can take the place of an enthusiastic teacher, a print-rich environment, and daily reading times. However, the materials provided in each section should help create a positive learning environment in which preschoolers may build on their prior knowledge while engaging in activities that meet their varied learning styles. Have fun!

# Reading Skills Overview

## Phonemic Awareness

Phonemic awareness is a subcategory of phonological awareness dealing with letter-sound association. Phonemic awareness activities include rhymes and phonemic patterns.

*Objective:* Students will learn about language sounds, sound positions, sound patterns, blending syllables, and word formation.

## Environmental Print

Environmental print consists of the letters, words, and symbols found in our home, school, and community. Environmental letters and words are the first symbols recognized by toddlers.

*Objective:* Students will be able to read and understand different symbols and words and their meanings.

## Visual Discrimination

Visual discrimination is the ability to see the likenesses and differences in colors, shapes, sizes, and letters. Through visual discrimination exercises, students understand about size and pattern and how it will aid them in forming the individual letters of the alphabet.

*Objective:* Students will learn to discriminate different letters using the concepts of color, shape, and size.

## Concepts of Print

Concepts of print include proper book handling, left-to-right reading directionality, and the difference between letters, words, and sentences.

*Objective:* Students will learn about book parts and the patterns used by authors as they record thoughts using letters and words.

## Alphabet

The alphabet consists of 26 letter symbols. Teachers often coordinate letter activities with curriculum themes. For example, the letter **A** is taught incorporating an apple theme, and the letter **I** is taught with an insect theme. Alphabet letter and sound recognition is a predictor of early reading success.

*Objective:* Students will learn to recognize letter symbols.

## Phonics

Phonics is the relationship between letters and sounds. Phonics is the system used to help decode words through memorization and identifying spelling patterns.

*Objective:* Students will understand the letter-sound relationship in order to read.

## Fine Motor Skills

Fine motor skills are developed through hands-on activities designed to strengthen the hand and arm muscles. Tools commonly used include pencils, crayons, markers, and manipulatives.

*Objective:* Students will experience a variety of hands-on activities to promote strengthening the small muscles in their fingers, hands, wrists, and arms.

# Phonemic Awareness

*Phonemic awareness* is a subcategory of phonological awareness that deals with letter-sound association. It is the recognition of spoken words or syllables made up of phonemes—the smallest units of sound that can be heard in any language (e.g., /b/ and /p/).

The development of phonemic awareness begins at birth when babies first hear their families' voices. As they grow, children learn to sing songs, recite rhymes, and listen to books read to them.

Phonemic awareness is an auditory skill. In theory, it could be taught in the dark by listening to letter sounds, hearing the distinction among letter sounds, counting syllables, and hearing and identifying similar sound and word patterns. Phonemic awareness is divided into three sections—Rhyming, Sound Positions, and Blending Sounds.

## Phonemic Awareness Assessment

A Phonemic Awareness Assessment is included on pages 79–80. Make a copy of page 79 for each student. Make only one copy of the picture page (page 80). Show each student the pictures and ask questions as outlined on page 79. Mark each student's responses on the page and add it to the student's portfolio.

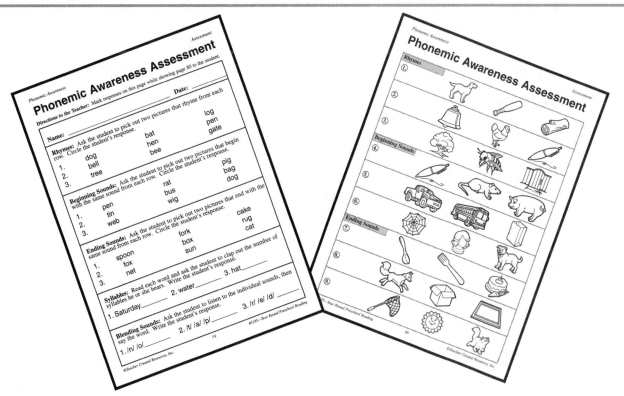

# Rhyming Activities

A *rhyming* word is a word that has the same ending sound as another word. *Hat* rhymes with *bat* and *cat* because the ending sounds are the same. Rhyming words are frequently used in poetry. The use of nursery rhymes and other poetry is an excellent way to teach students to listen for sounds. The following activities provide practice identifying and articulating rhyming words.

## Rhyme Poster Activity

**Preparation:** Copy the Picture Cards (pages 12, 20, 27, 34) and Word Cards (pages 13–18, 21–25, 28–32, 35–41). Enlarge the Rhyme Posters (pages 11, 19, 26, and 33) for use with students. Cut out the Picture Cards and Word Cards and laminate.

### Directions

1. Share a Rhyme Poster with the students, and track the print as you read it.
2. Ask the students to point out the rhyming words.
3. Next, have the students clap the rhythms of each line.
4. Place the Word Cards in a pocket chart. Read each word aloud to the students. Add the appropriate punctuation to the poem using the cards on page 41.
5. Then have the students replace the Word Cards with the Rhyme Picture Cards.

## Additional Rhyme Activities

1. Replace words in other familiar rhymes, poems, or songs (e.g., "If you're happy and you know it, clap your hands," may be substituted with "If you're happy and you know it, rub your belly.").
2. Make a class book incorporating the song "Hey There, Hey Now." (See pages 7–8.)
3. Place the following Picture Cards (pages 49–74) on the floor: fan-can, pear-bear, cat-hat, box-fox, hug-rug, wig-pig, and mop-top. Have the students match the rhyming cards.
4. Have a Rhyme Find. Instruct the students to look for objects in the room that rhyme with bear (chair), pink (sink), cord (board), dart (chart), toy (boy), curl (girl), and roar (floor/door).
5. Create a Class Rhyme Book using rhyming objects each student has brought from home. (See pages 9–10.)

# Rhyming Activities *(cont.)*

Practice singing the rhyming song below before beginning the Hey There, Hey Now Class Book. Discuss the rhyming words at the end of each line. Mention that the class will be taking turns making rhyming words using their own names. Once students are familiar with the lyrics, take turns substituting each student's name in the place of *me* in the song and a rhyming word beginning with an /h/ in the place of *hee*.

## Hey There, Hey Now Class Book

### Materials

- 2 sheets of 9" x 12" construction paper
- copy of page 8 for each student
- photo of each student
- crayons or markers
- copy of the title page (below)

> ### Hey There, Hey Now
> *(Sing to the tune of "Willoughby Wallaby")*
>
> Hey there, hey now hee,
> An octopus hung on me.
> Hey there, hey now hoo,
> An octopus hung on you.
>
> *Example:* Hey there, hey now *Harmen*
> An octopus hung on *Karmen*.

### Directions

1. Have each child place his or her photo (or draw one) in the box on page 8.
2. Encourage each child to write his or her name on the first line. Then help find a word that rhymes with his or her name. In many cases, this word will be a nonsense word. Write the word on the line provided.
3. Have each child color the octopus above his or her picture.
4. Use construction paper to create the cover and back of the book. Glue the title page to the front.
5. Add the pages for each student.
6. Bind the book. Thin books may be stapled while thicker books may be bound using O-rings or a binding machine. Share the book with the class and display it for future readings.

# Hey There, Hey Now

Hey there, hey now _____,

An octopus hung on _____.

Hey there, hey now hoo,

An octopus hung on you.

# Rhyming Activities *(cont.)*

This creative rhyming book takes only a bit of preparation! Have each student bring two objects that rhyme from home. Suggest to parents that they send objects large enough to see in a picture but not too big to fit in a student book bag.

## Class Rhyme Book

### Materials

- 2 sheets of 9" x 12" construction paper
- photo of each student holding 2 objects
- copy of page 10 for each student
- glue

### Directions

1. Take a picture of each student with his or her objects (one in each hand).

2. Glue each student's picture on a copy of page 10. Write the child's name and the name of the two objects that rhyme. Or have the child draw two objects that rhyme on a sheet of paper.

3. Create a title page using one piece of construction paper. Assemble the pages as desired. Use the second piece of construction paper for the back of the book.

4. Bind the book. Thin books may be stapled while thicker books may be bound using O-rings or a binding machine.

Kristin's rhymes are cat and hat.

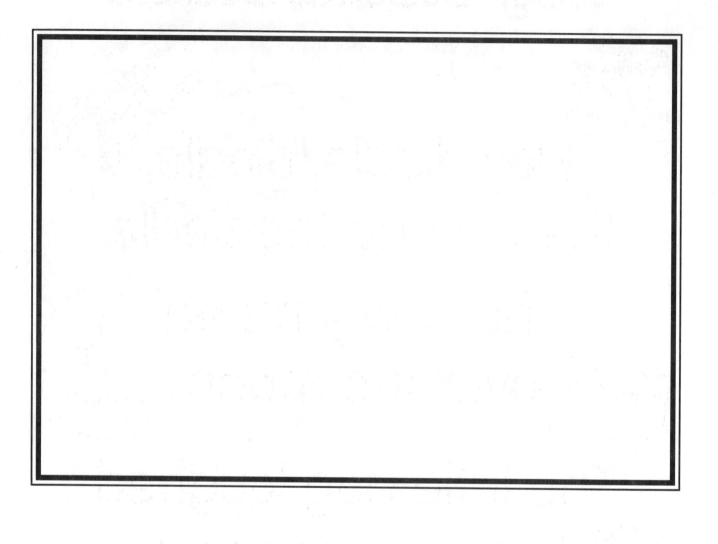

_____'s **rhymes**

**are** _____ **and** _____.

# Hey Diddle, Diddle

Hey diddle, diddle,
the cat and the fiddle,

the cow jumped
over the moon.

The little dog laughed
to see such sport,

and the dish ran away
with the spoon!

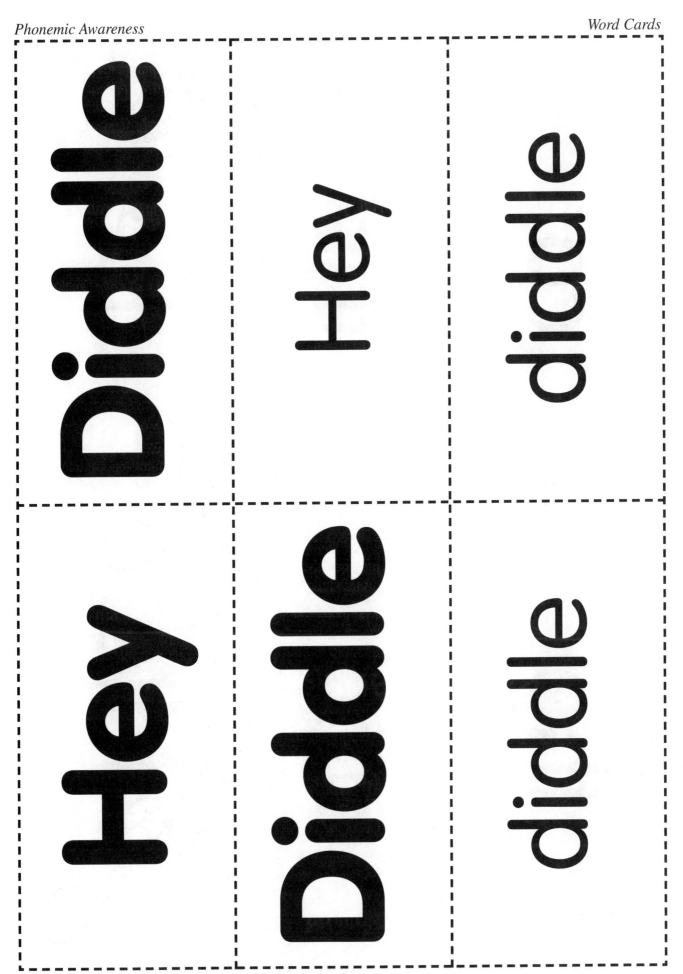

**Diddle**

**Hey**

**diddle**

**Hey**

**Diddle**

**diddle**

cat

the

the

the

and

fiddle

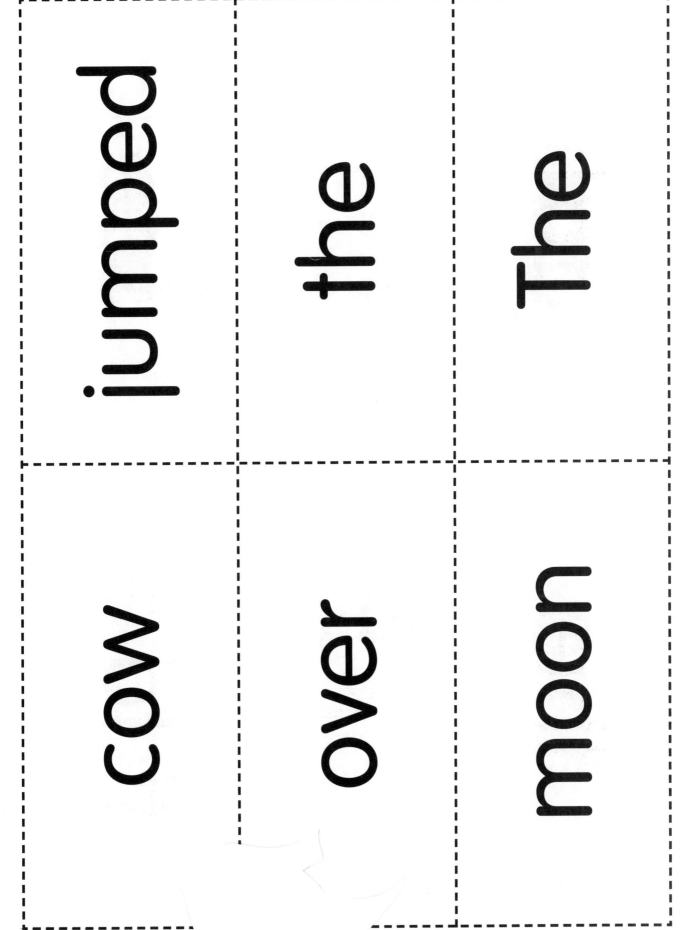

jumped

the

The

cow

over

moon

dog

see

laughed

little

to

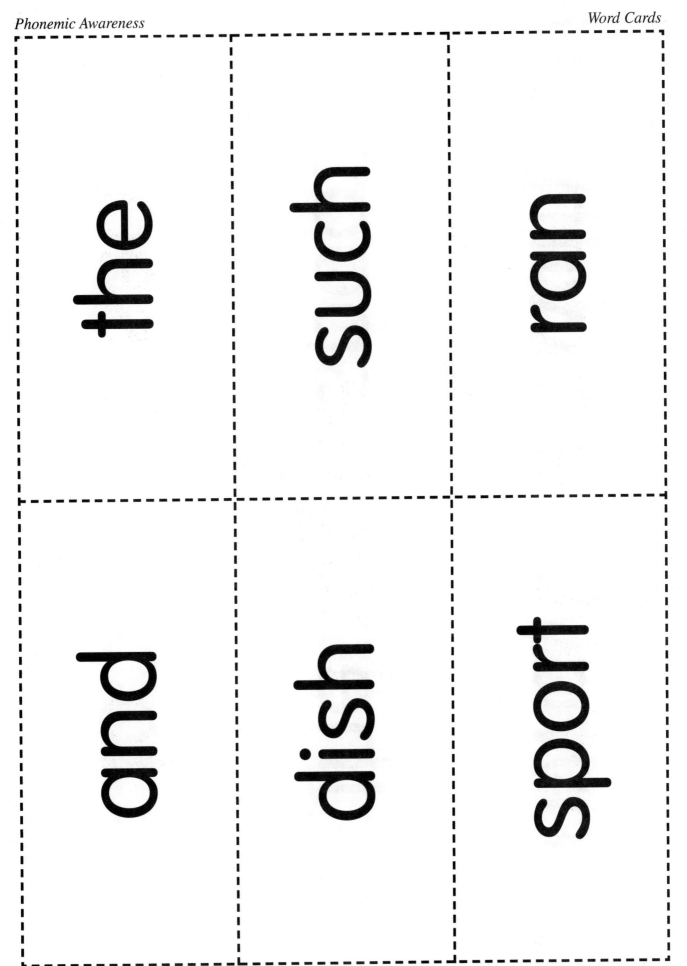

the

such

ran

and

dish

sport

with

spoon

away

the

# Little Miss Muffet

Little Miss Muffet
sat on a tuffet,
eating her curds and whey.
Along came a spider,
who sat down beside her,
and frightened
Miss Muffet away.

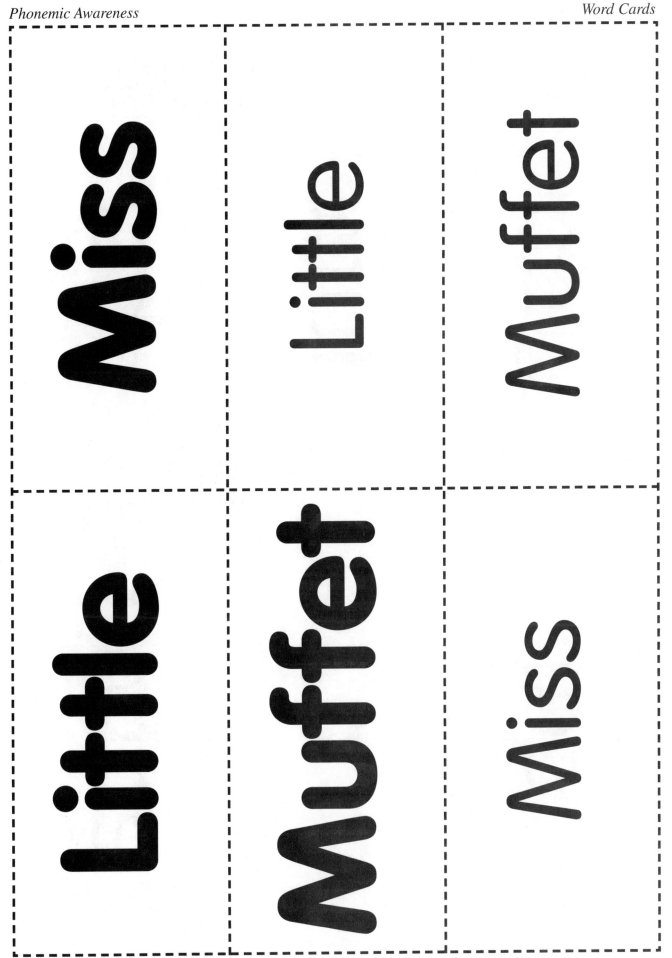

on

tuffet

her

sat

a

eating

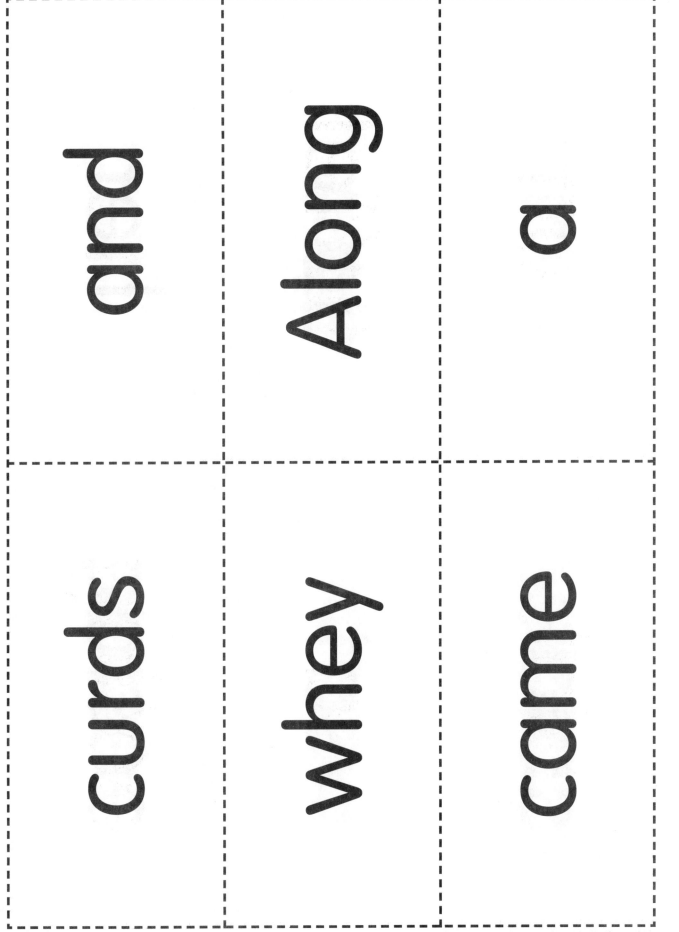

and

Along

a

curds

whey

came

who

down

her

spider

sat

beside

Miss

away

frightened

and

Muffet

# Jack and Jill

Jack and Jill
went up the hill
to fetch a pail of water.
Jack fell down,
and broke his crown,
and Jill came tumbling after.

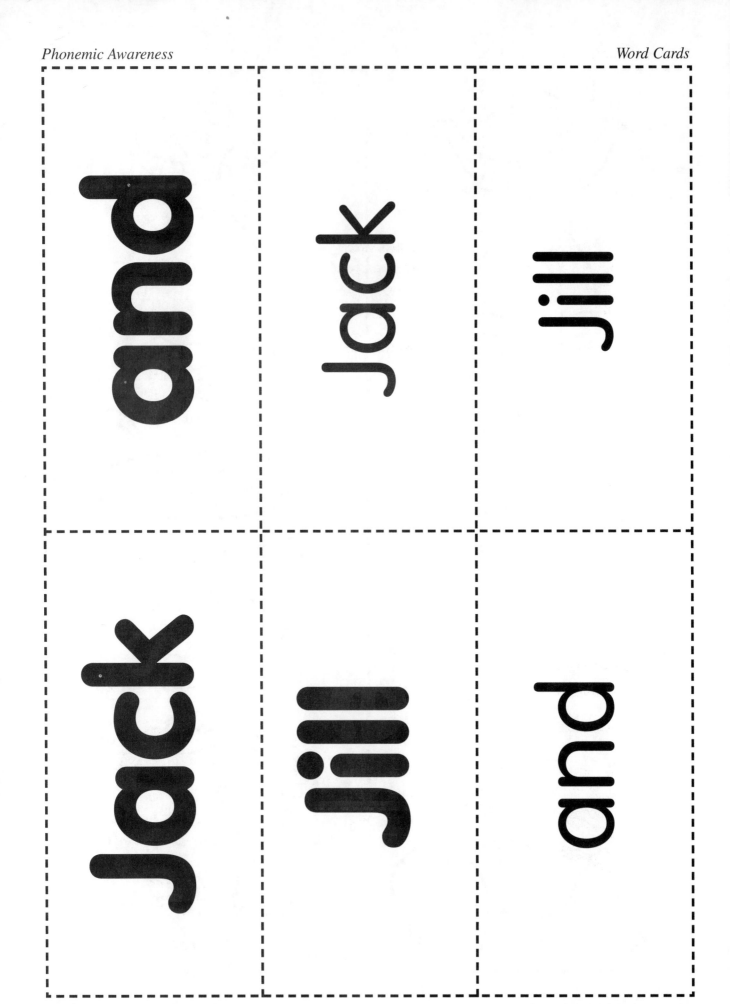

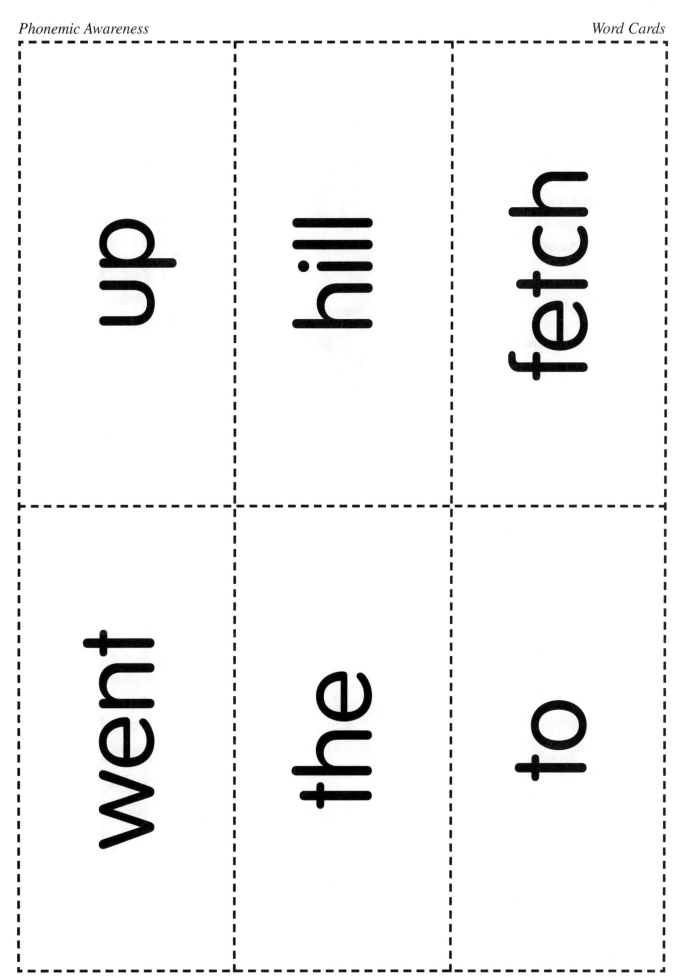

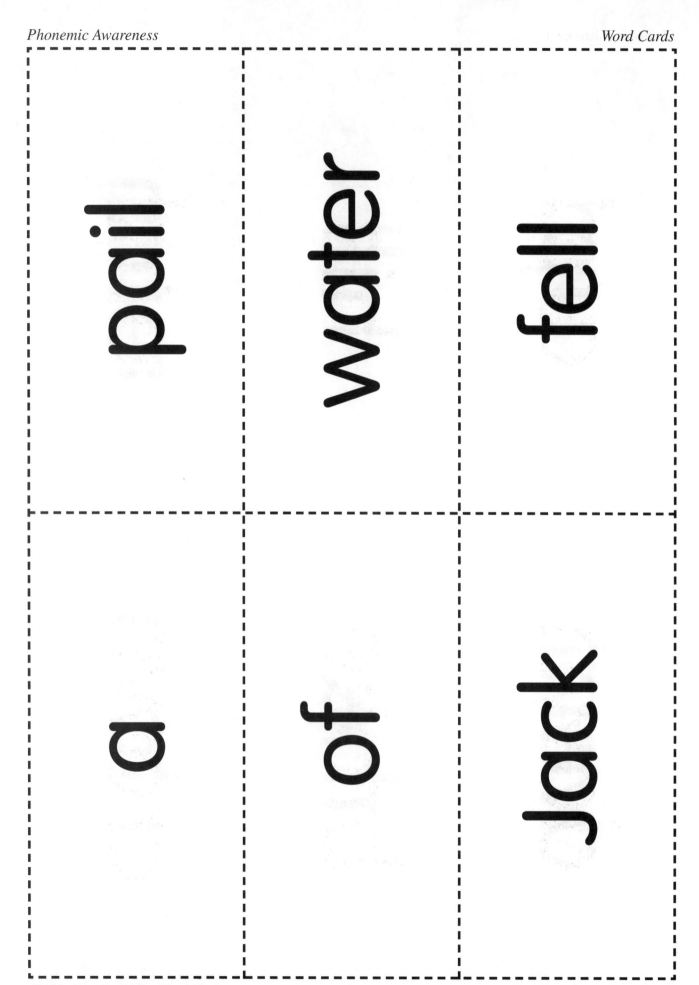

pail

water

fell

a

of

Jack

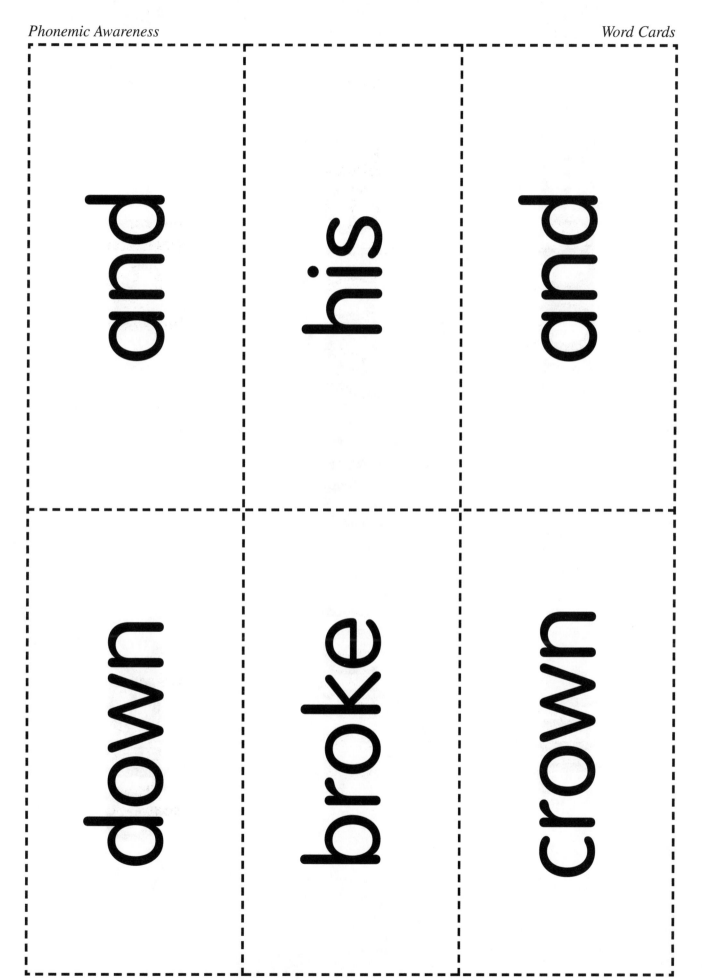

and

his

and

down

broke

crown

came

Jill

tumbling

after

# One, Two, Buckle My Shoe

1, 2, buckle my shoe.

3, 4, shut the door.

5, 6, pick up sticks.

7, 8, lay them straight.

9, 10, a big fat hen!

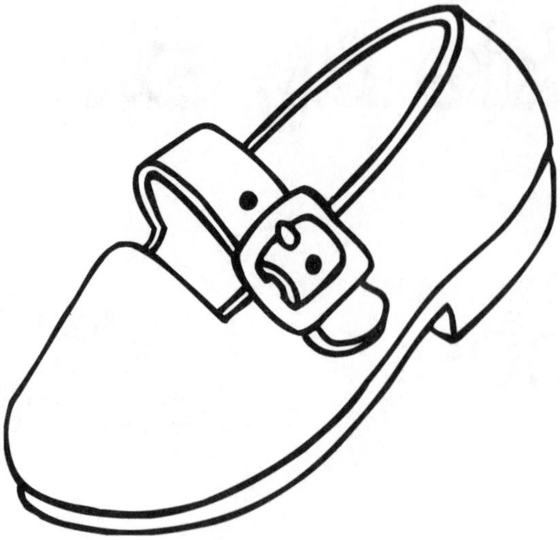
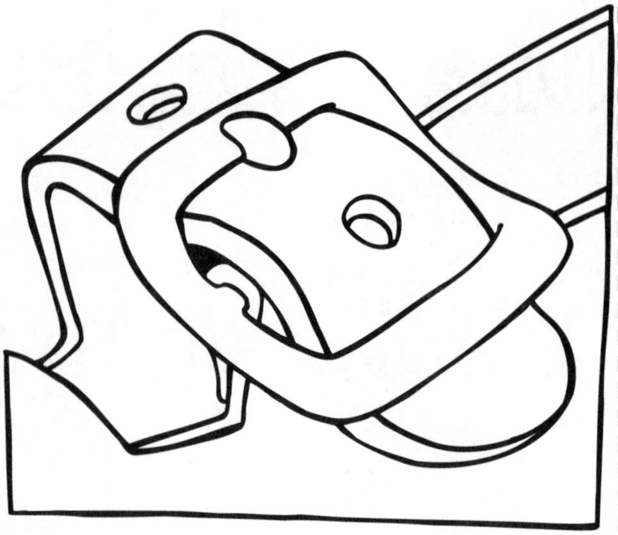
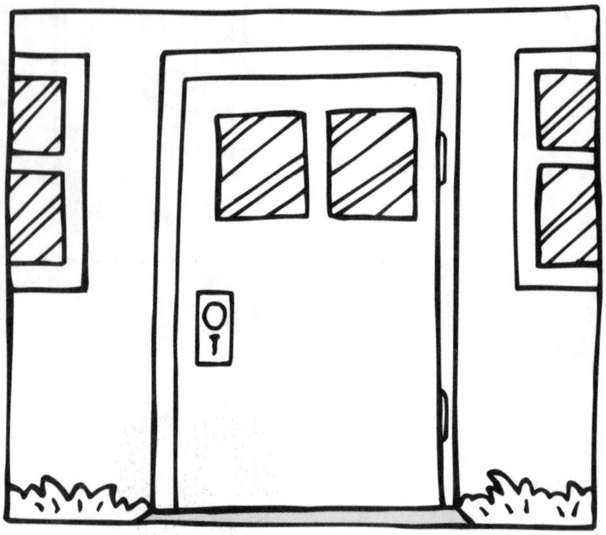
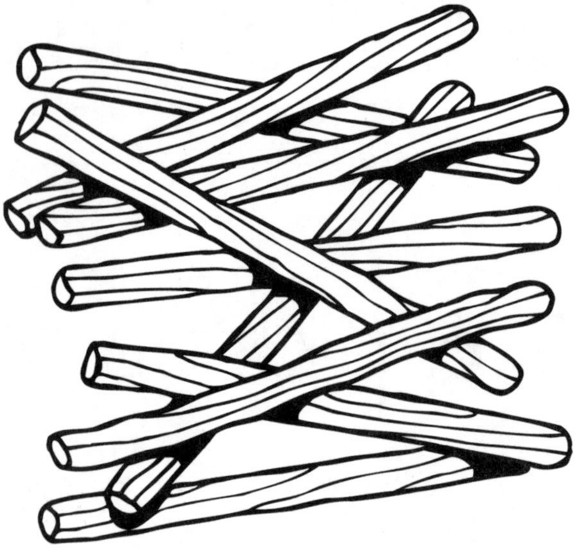
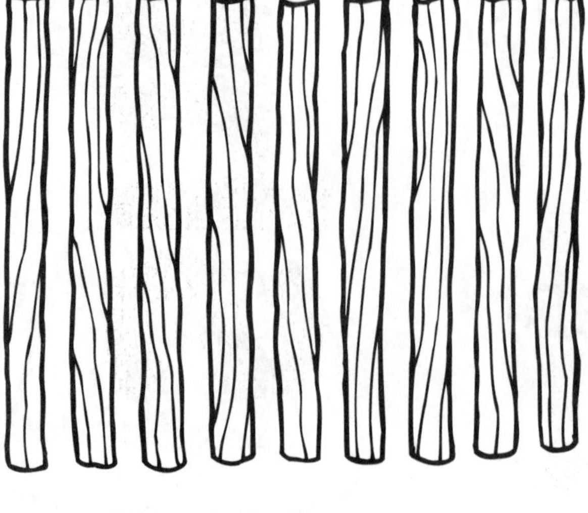
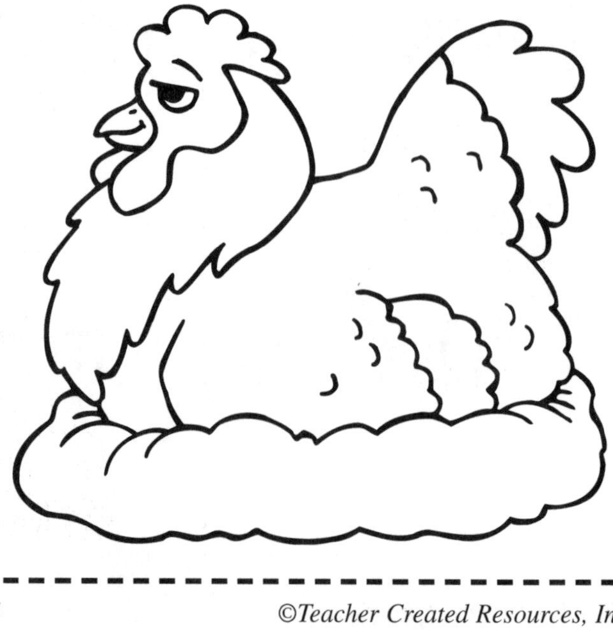

 

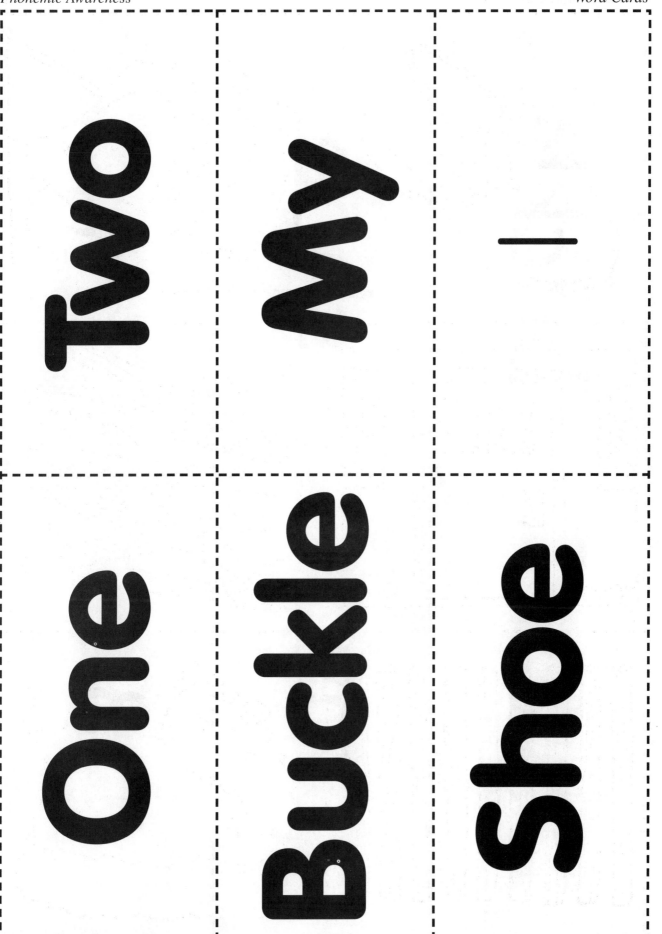

Two

My

I

One

Buckle

Shoe

buckle

shoe

4

2

my

3

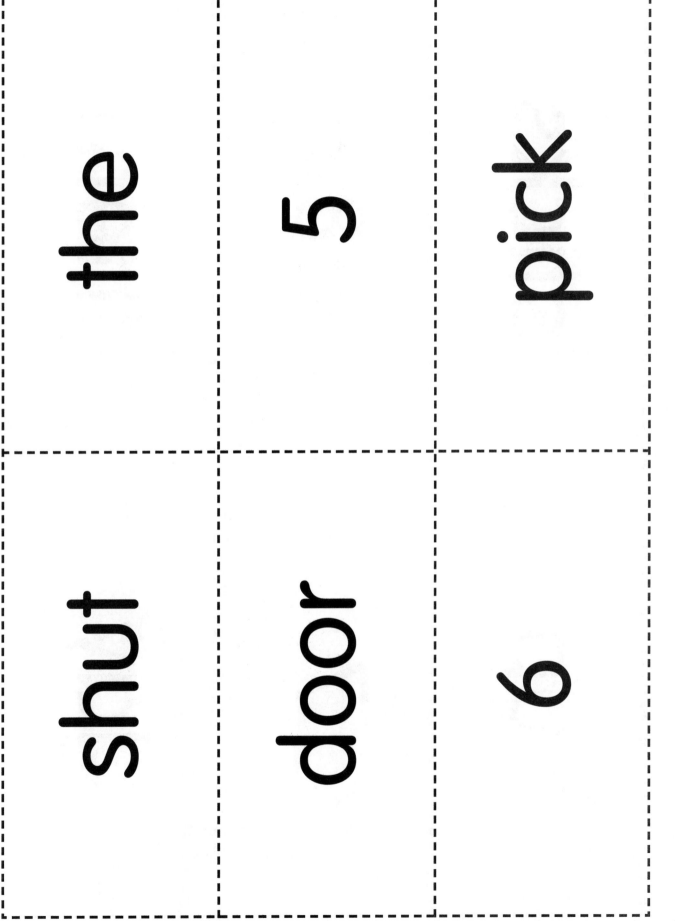

the

5

pick

shut

door

6

sticks

8

them

up

7

lay

9

a

straight

10

fat

big

hen

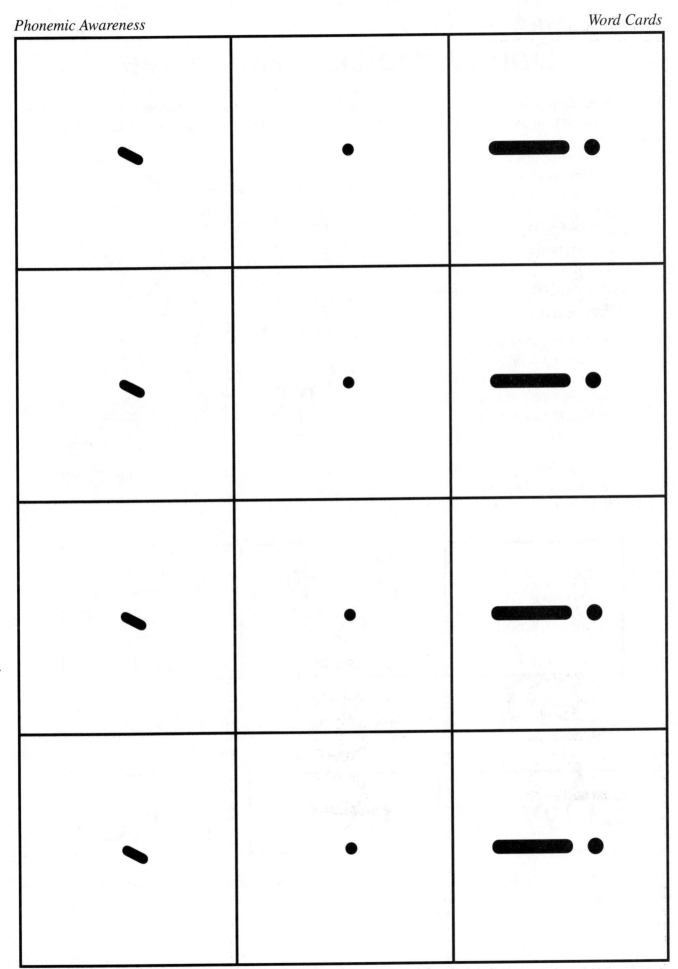

# Sound Position Activities

The terms *beginning*, *middle*, and *end* need to be understood by each student before teaching the sounds and their positions in words. The activities below will help reinforce the concept of beginning, middle and end.

1. Place three objects in a row and discuss which object is at the beginning, middle, and end. Always work from the left to right when pointing to a series of objects. This will reinforce the manner in which we approach a page we are planning to read.

2. Line up three students and talk about which person is at the beginning of the line, the middle of the line, and the end of the line. Rearrange the students and ask the questions again.

3. Position any three Picture Cards (pages 49–74) in a row and ask the students to identify which picture is in the *beginning*, *middle*, and *ending* position.

ant        bear        bed

4. Organize three Word Cards (pages 43–44), or write three words in a row on the chalkboard and ask the students to identify which word is in the *beginning*, *middle*, and *ending* position.

cow        cat        hat

5. Use the Word Cards (pages 43–44) to create three sentences, or write three of your own sentences on the chalkboard, and ask which sentence is in the *beginning*, *middle*, and *ending* position.

dog

we

toys.

The

sat.

like

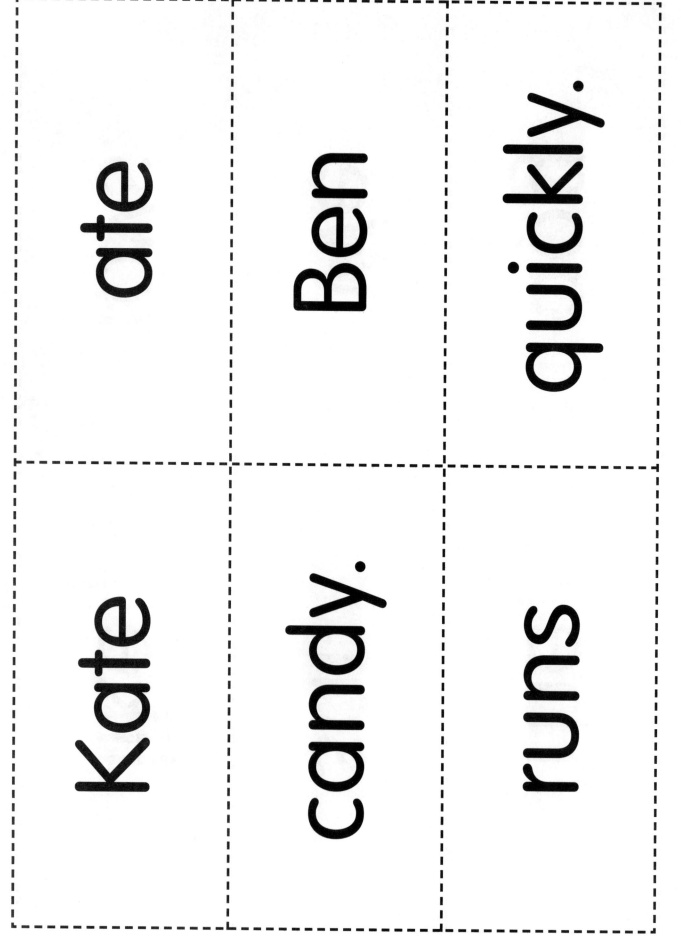

ate

Ben

quickly.

Kate

candy.

runs

# Beginning Sound Activities

Learning beginning sounds helps children make the first, vital connection between letters in the alphabet and the sounds they represent in words. These activities concentrate on letter sounds found at the beginning of a word.

1. Use the Picture Cards (pages 49–74). Pick two cards that begin with the same sound and one that does not. Display the three cards. Then, ask the students to determine which two cards begin with the same sound. Try the following combinations: jar, jam, kite; queen, rug, quilt; egg, inchworm, envelope; octopus, ox, noodle; and lamb, log, mop.

  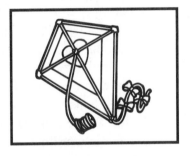

2. Most students know the beginning letter in their first name. Go over the beginning sound in each student's name. Example: /D/, /D/, Damian, /K/, /K/, Kirstin, /E/, /E/, Ellen, /D/, /D/, David.

3. Show the Picture Cards (pages 49–74). Go over the beginning sound in each of these pictures. You may begin by saying, "This is an /m/, /m/, mop; this is a /c/, /c/, can; this is a /w/, /w/, wig; and this is a /p/, /p/, pig." After the students understand this concept, hold up the cards. Ask them what beginning sound their lips make when they say the word associated with the picture card. The students will respond by saying, "That is a /h/, /h/ hat."

4. Point at objects in the classroom while saying, "This is a /t/, /t/, television; this is a /d/, /d/, desk; this is a /c/, /c/, computer."

5. Play Thumbs Up, Thumbs Down. Make enough copies on card stock of the Thumbs Up, Thumbs Down page (page 47) to supply one hand per student.

Hold up a Picture Card (pages 49–74) and ask the students if it begins with an /m/ sound. If it does, the students respond by pointing the thumb up. If the card does not begin with an /m/ sound, then the students show the thumb pointing down. Continue playing until all the cards have been viewed.

# Ending Sound Activities

An ending sound is the last identifiable sound within a word. These activities help move students who can identify all letter sounds one step closer to reading by helping them listen for words that have the same ending sound.

1. Point at objects in the classroom while saying, "This is a sink, /k/, /k/; this is a rug, /g/, /g/; this is a pencil, /l/, /l/."

2. Show the Picture Cards (pages 49–74). Go over the ending sound in each of these pictures. You may begin by saying, "This is a bed, /d/, /d/; this is a game, /m/, /m/; and this is a moon, /n/, /n/." After the students understand this concept, hold up the cards. Ask them what ending sound their lips make when they say the word associated with the picture card. The students will respond by saying, "That is a vase, /s/, /s/." **Note:** While it is true that some picture cards end in *e*, the teacher is working only on sounds and not spelling in this part of the lesson.

3. Play Thumbs Up, Thumbs Down. Make copies of the Thumbs Up, Thumbs Down cards (page 47} on cardstock. Hold up a Picture Card (pages 49–74) and ask the students if it ends with an /m/. If it does, the students respond by pointing the thumb up. If the card does not end with an /m/, then the students show the thumb pointing down.

4. Use the Picture Cards (pages 49–74). Pick two cards that end with the same sound and one that does not. Display the three cards. Then, ask the students to determine which two cards end with the same sound. Try the following combinations: *rug, egg, mop; inchworm, jam, ox;* and *kite, quilt, noodle.*

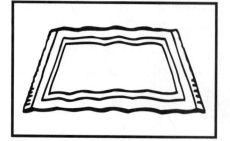  

## Middle Sounds

Middle sounds may be taught using the beginning and ending sound activities. The middle sound lessons can be taught using only three-letter words at this stage of development. Do not assess middle sounds if students are not developmentally ready.

# Thumbs Up, Thumbs Down

**Directions:** Cut out the hands and attach them to craft sticks. Practice flipping the hands to signal "thumbs up" or "thumbs down."

# Blending Sounds Activities

A *syllable* is a segment of speech with at least one vowel. There are many rules for dividing words into syllables. However, preschoolers need only use auditory skills to clap the number of syllables. These activities will help students recognize the number of syllables within a word.

1. Clap syllables in a student's name and count them. Example: Say and clap, "Lew-is." Then tell the students that Lewis has two syllables.

2. Clap and say the number of syllables in the names of objects around the room: pro-jec-tor, desk, tel-e-vi-sion, pen-cil.

3. Use the Picture Cards (pages 49–74). Clap the syllables in each word: ap-ple, inch-worm, ring, ox, um-brel-la, and yo-yo.

4. Use the Syllable Cards (pages 75–78). Have the students tell you how many syllables are in the words: ba-na-na, mon-ster, el-e-phant, air-plane, but-ter-fly, tel-e-vi-sion, hip-po-pot-a-mus, com-put-er.

5. Demonstrate how the students may blend syllables. Accentuate the individual syllables as you slowly say a word. Have the students respond by saying the word. For example, the teacher says, "oat-meal," and the students respond by saying, "oatmeal." The teacher says, "win-dow," and the students respond by saying "window."

6. Use the Picture Cards (pages 49–74). Have the children listen for the individual sounds within a group of words and blend them to form the words as you say them. Example: You say /d/ /o/ /g/, and they say *dog*. You say /e/ /g/, and they say *egg*.

7. If the students are developmentally ready, sound out each letter of a word and ask the students to respond with the word. The teacher may say /l/ /o/ /g/, and the students will respond by saying *log*.

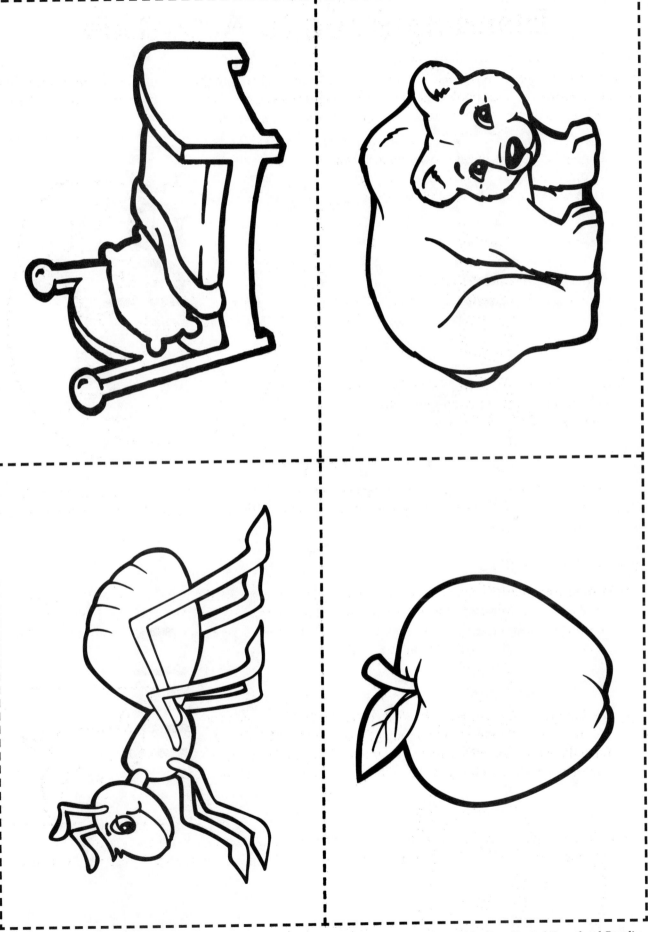

bear

bed

apple

ant

dog

door

can

cat

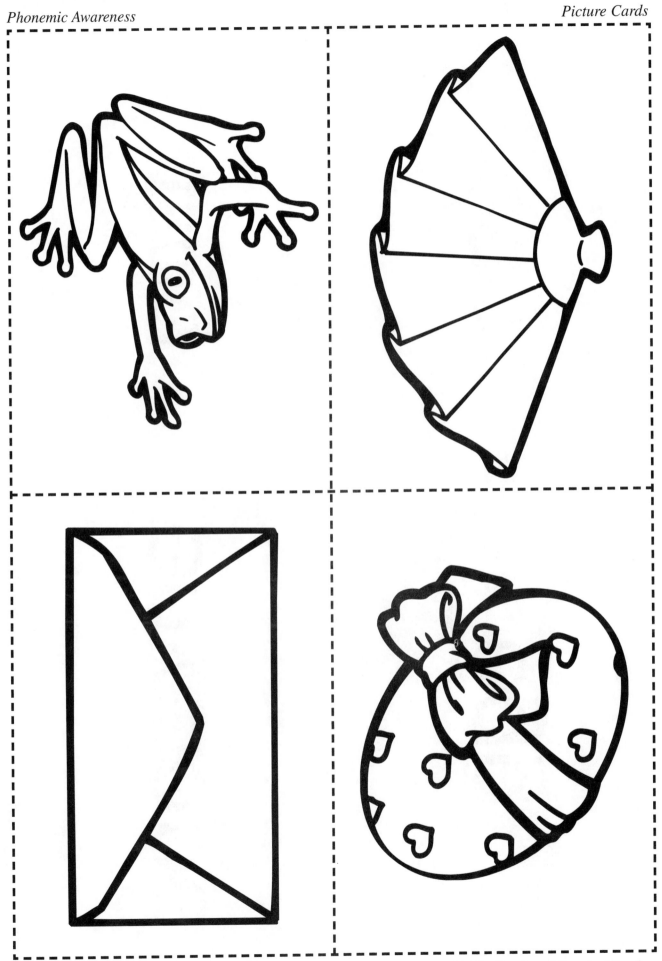

fan

frog

egg

envelope

hose

hat

goat

game

56

jam

jar

inchworm

insect

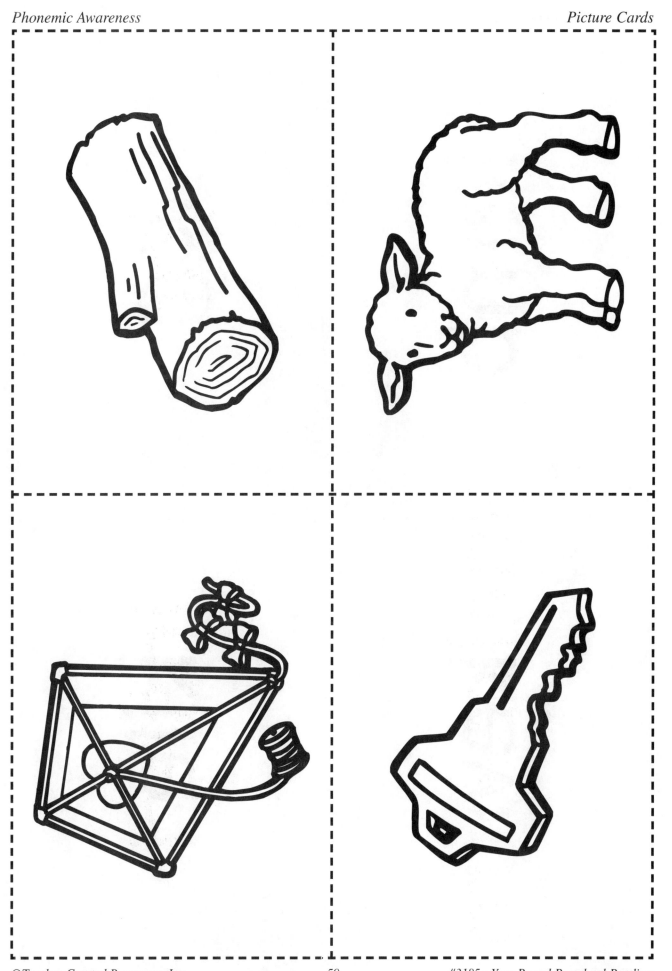

lamb

log

key

kite

nail

nest

moon

mop

pear

pig

octopus

ox

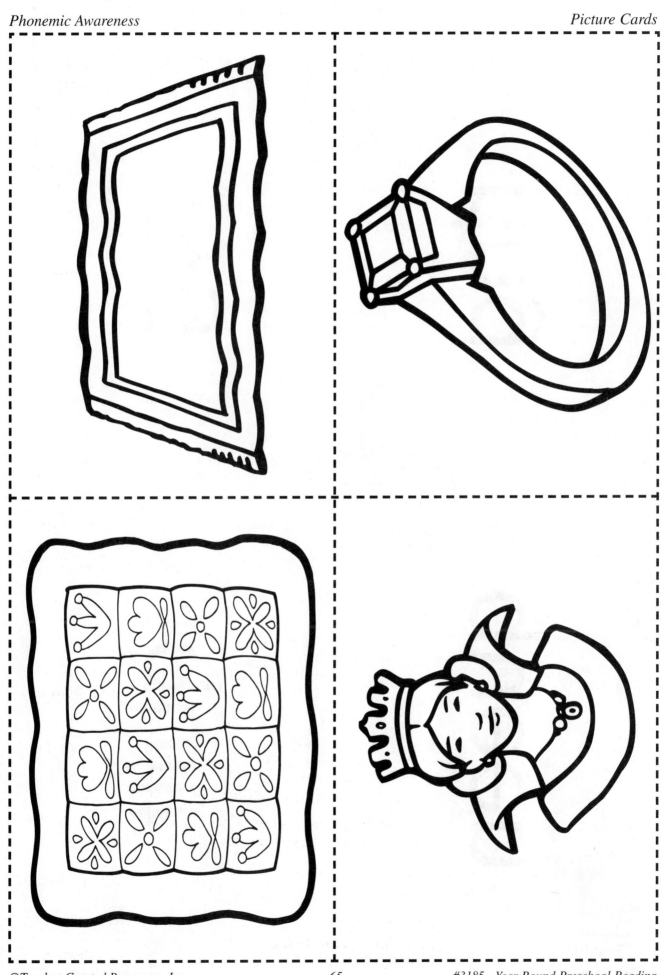

ring

rug

queen

quilt

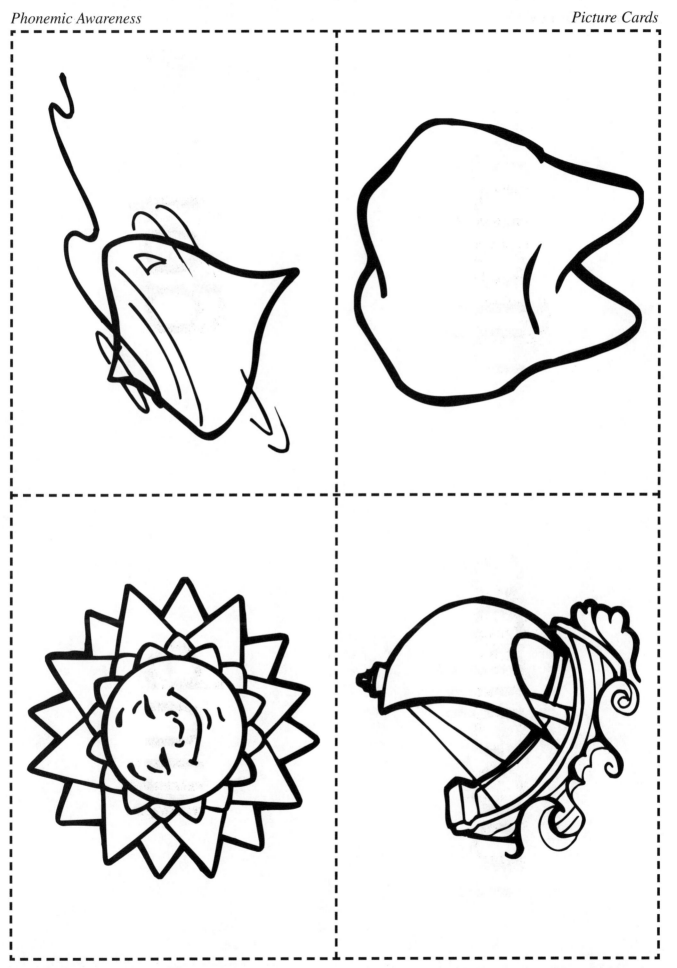

tooth

top

sailboat

sun

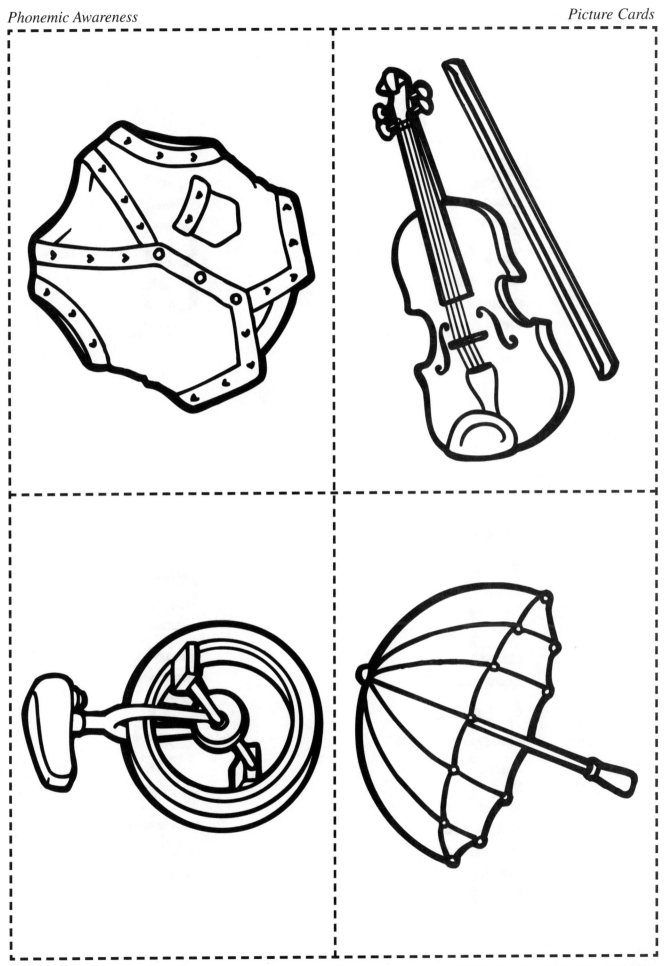

violin

vest

umbrella

unicycle

fox

box

wagon

wig

zebra

zipper

yarn

yo-yo

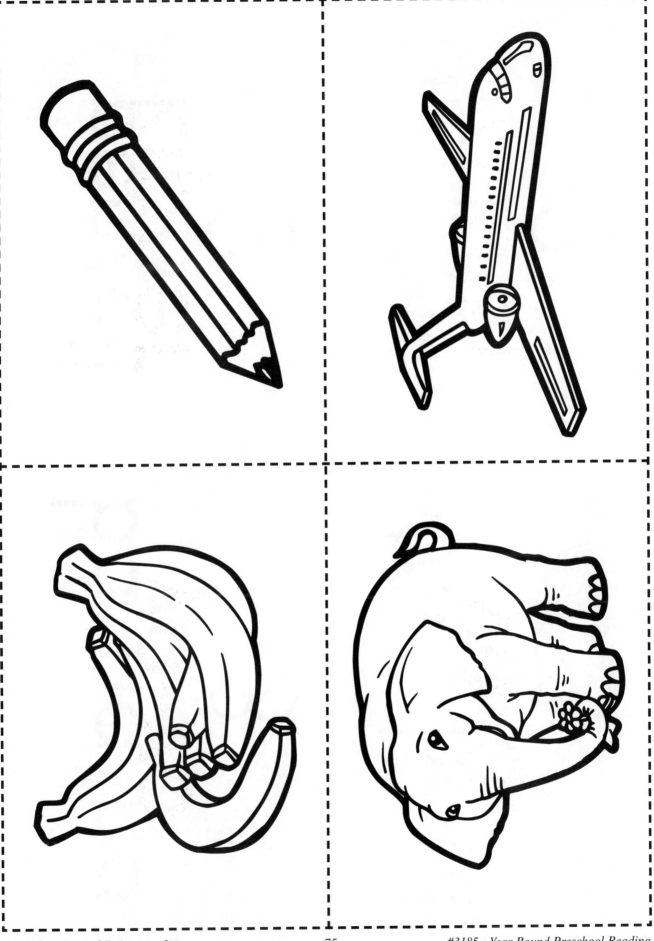

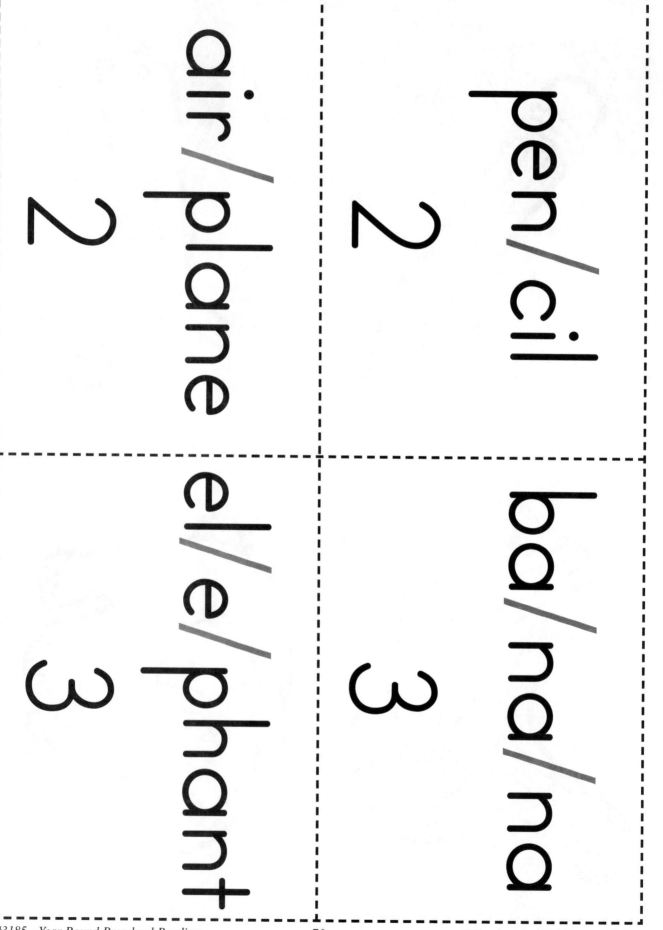

pen/cil

2

air/plane

2

ba/na/na

3

el/e/phant

3

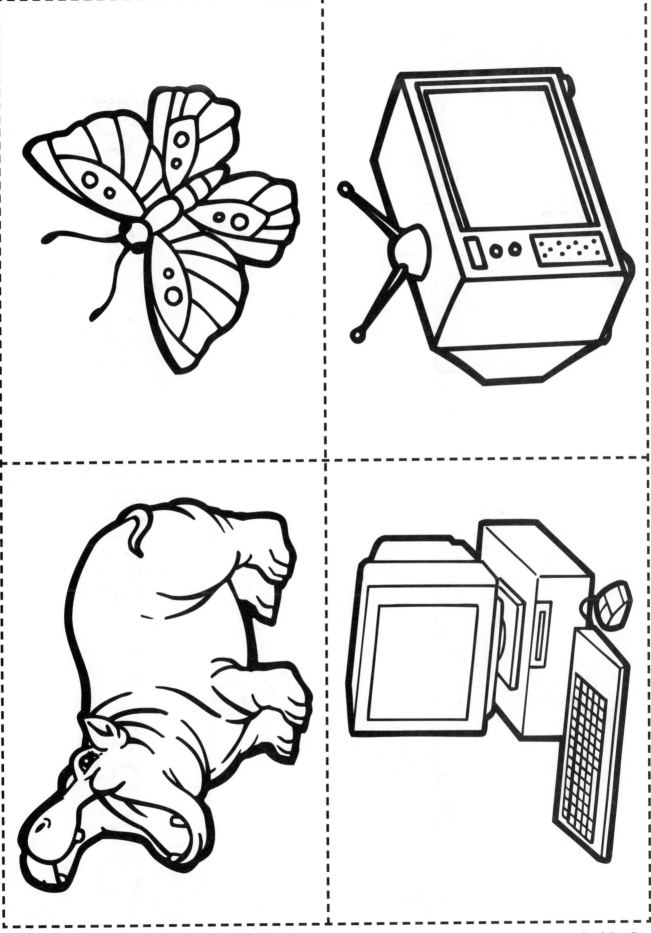

but/ter/fly

3

hip/po/pot/a/mus

5

tel/e/vi/sion

4

com/pu/ter

3

# Phonemic Awareness Assessment

**Directions to the Teacher:** Mark responses on this page while showing page 80 to the student.

| Name: | Date: |
|---|---|

**Rhymes:** Ask the student to pick out two pictures that rhyme from each row. Circle the student's response.

| | | |
|---|---|---|
| 1. | dog | bat | log |
| 2. | bell | hen | pen |
| 3. | tree | bee | gate |

**Beginning Sounds:** Ask the student to pick out two pictures that begin with the same sound from each row. Circle the student's response.

| 1. | pen | rat | pig |
|---|---|---|---|
| 2. | truck | bus | bag |
| 3. | web | wig | dog |

**Ending Sounds:** Ask the student to pick out two pictures that end with the same sound from each row. Circle the student's response.

| 1. | spoon | fork | cake |
|---|---|---|---|
| 2. | fox | box | rug |
| 3. | net | sun | cat |

**Syllables:** Read each word and ask the student to clap out the number of syllables he or she hears. Write the student's response.

1. Saturday_____     2. water_____     3. hat_____

**Blending Sounds:** Ask the student to listen to the individual sounds, then say the word. Write the student's response.

1. /n/ /o/_____     2. /t/ /a/ /p/_____     3. /r/ /e/ /d/ _____

# Phonemic Awareness Assessment *(cont.)*

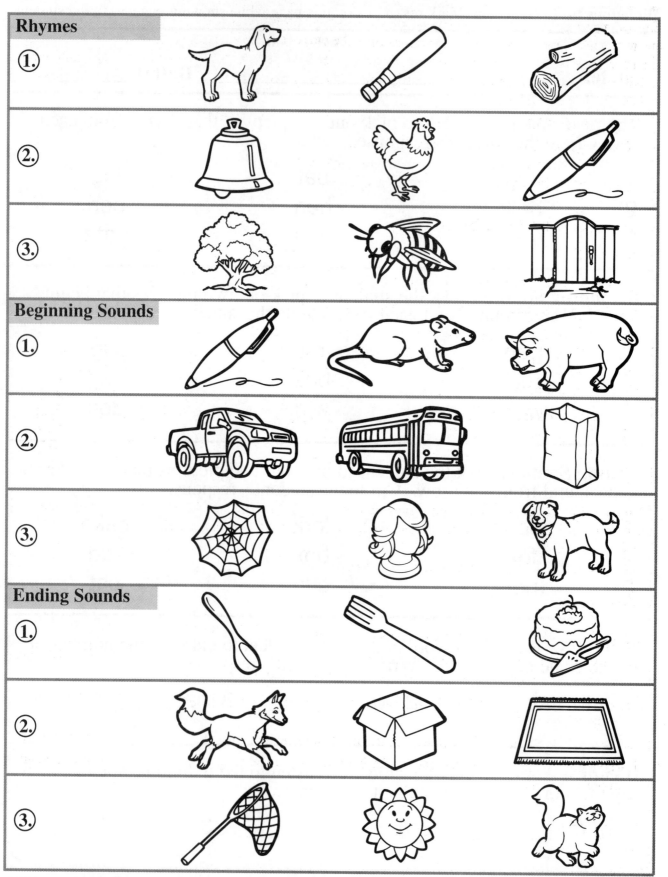

**Rhymes**

①.

②.

③.

**Beginning Sounds**

①.

②.

③.

**Ending Sounds**

①.

②.

③.

# Environmental Print Activities

*Environmental print* includes the letters, words, and symbols found in home, school, and community environments. Displaying environmental print in the classroom helps children feel successful "reading" at an early age. These early successes motivate young children to read more and more. The following activities will expose your preschoolers to a variety of environmental print and build their awareness and confidence in reading.

1. Create a class Environmental Print Book. (Directions are provided below.) This activity works well with thematic studies on local communities or community helpers. It creates an excellent opportunity for parents to become involved in their child's learning.

## Environmental Print Book

### Materials

- copy of home letter (page 83) for each student
- copy of book page (page 84) for each student
- copy of cover page (page 84)
- sheet of cardstock
- objects from home
- glue and scissors
- hole-punch
- yarn or ribbon

**Preparation:** Copy the home letter (page 83), fill in the due date, and have students sign the letter asking their parents to help them collect environmental print examples. Send the letter home in the students' book bags at least one week before beginning this activity. Copy the cover page (page 84) onto cardstock. Copy the book page (page 84) for each student.

### Directions

1. Ask the students to share the examples of environmental print they collected.
2. Observe the students' reactions to the print and select the top 10 or 15 pieces (one per student) to use to make an environmental print book for the classroom library.
3. Give each student a copy of page 84. Allow him or her to cut and paste the environmental print sample on the page.
4. Assemble the book by hole punching the left-hand side and tying it together with yarn or ribbon.
5. Have the students take turns reading the book to the class each day until all students have had an opportunity to read.

# Environmental Print Activities *(cont.)*

2. Using the Environmental Print Cards (page 85), play an identification game with students as a whole class or in small groups. Ask, "Which sign shows where it is safe to cross the street?" Have a student point to the correct sign.

3. Make an environmental print dictionary and collect examples for each letter of the alphabet.

4. Create an environmental print puzzle. Have students bring in duplicate samples of prepared food boxes such as cereal, cakes, and crackers. Set aside one of each pair of boxes. Then cut the faces of the other boxes into different-sized puzzle pieces. Tape the duplicate food box, which was set aside, to a plastic bag. Store the corresponding puzzle pieces in that bag.

---

**Environmental Print Assessment**

For an Environmental Print Assessment, ask students to identify environmental print they recognize within the school, or have students point out environmental print in the Environmental Print Book or the Environmental Print Cards.

---

Date: _____

Hello,

Next week, my class will begin a study on the people, places, and things I enjoy about my community. My teacher has asked me to collect examples of the letters, words, and symbols I see every day. My teacher says these letters, words, and symbols are called "environmental print." They are some of the first pieces of reading I will encounter as a preschooler. Environmental print includes trademarks used to represent products I might use and businesses I might go. Examples include names of food, toys, fast food restaurants, and local stores.

Please help me locate some symbols I can recognize and read independently. I will share them with my classmates on

_____.

My teacher said I may choose one symbol to appear in a class book on environmental print we will make together. I am really excited about working with you on this assignment!

Sincerely,

_____

I can read . . . .

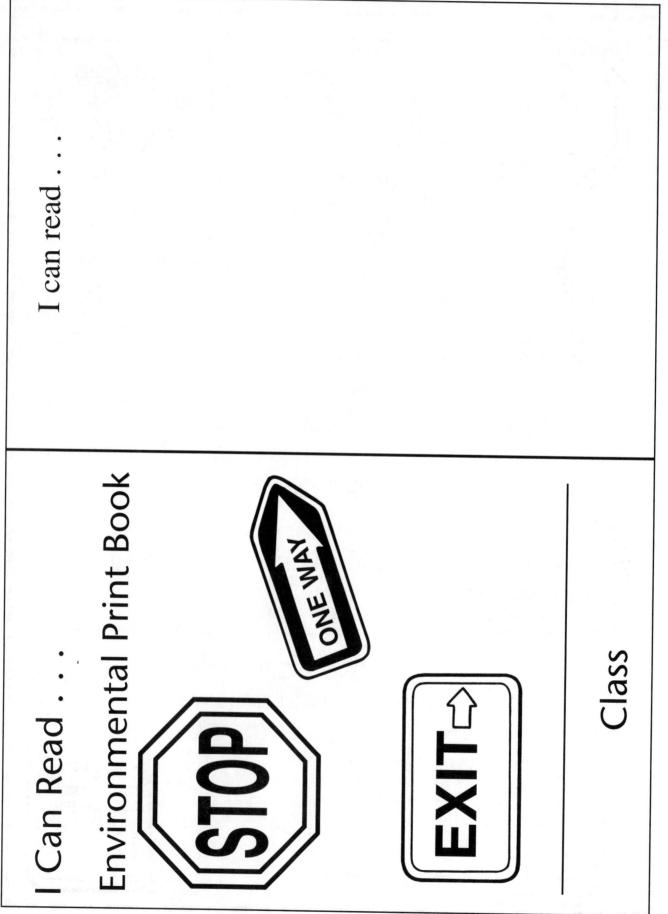

I Can Read . . . .
Environmental Print Book

STOP

ONE WAY

EXIT

Class

# Shape, Size, and Color Activities

*Visual discrimination* refers to the ability to see the likenesses and differences in colors, shapes, sizes, and letters. The ability to visually discriminate letters and words is essential in learning to read. All printed letters are set against a certain background. The difference in the letters and the background is color. Thus, the first discrimination children understand is color. Then children discriminate letters using the concepts of shape and size.

## Shape Activities

1. Play the Shape Jump game using sidewalk chalk. Draw the different shapes your students are learning on the sidewalk or playground. Demonstrate how to play the game by jumping to a shape and naming it. Discuss the number of sides and corners of each shape. Expand the concept by asking the students to jump to the shape and name a letter this shape can be used to make. For example, a triangle is part of a capital A, a circle can be an O, a square looks like two L's put together, and a diamond looks like two V's put together.

2. Create a Shape Book using copies of pages 87–93. Have students find pictures of items in magazines, newspapers, or coloring books that contain each basic shape. Staple or bind the book together.

3. Write out each student's name (one at a time). As a class, look for recognizable shapes within each letter.

4. Do a Shape Hunt in the classroom. Locate objects in the classroom that relate to the different shapes. Example: door–rectangle, television–square, clock–circle, and door stop–triangle.

5. Using the Alphabet Cards (pages 134–138), sort the cards into two groups: uppercase and lowercase letters. (See directions for cards on page 132, number 12.)

## Size Activities

1. Create a classroom pictograph and organize the students by height from shortest to tallest (each foot could be one square; squares are equal-sized). Display the pictograph on the bulletin board to visually illustrate the different sizes.

2. Have students play a sorting game with manipulatives. Instruct the students to group the manipulatives according to size.

## Color Activities

Most students can recognize the basic colors when they come to preschool. However, teachers may modify the shape and size activities above to include sorting by color.

---

### Visual Discrimination Assessment: Shape, Size, and Color

Have each student organize manipulatives by shape (e.g., pattern blocks), size (e.g., adult, child, and baby socks), or color (e.g., Unifix® cubes).

---

# My Shape Book

By _____

Name: _____

Directions: Trace on the dotted line to form the diamond shape within the picture.

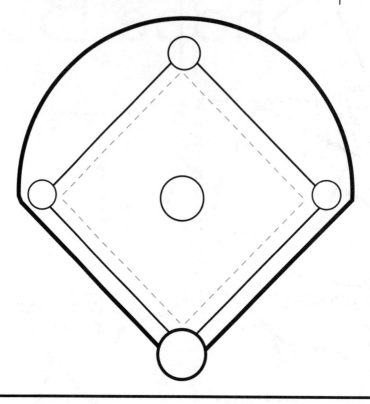

Directions: Draw a picture of an object shaped like a diamond or find a picture in a magazine and attach it to the page.

Diamond

88

Name: _____

Directions: Trace on the dotted lines to form the rectangle shapes within the picture.

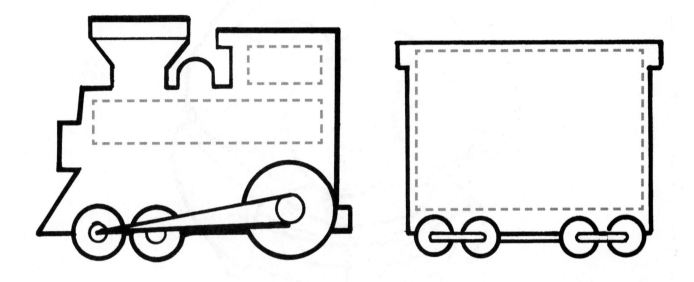

Directions: Draw a picture of an object shaped like a rectangle or find a picture in a magazine and attach it to the page.

Name: _____

Directions: Trace on the dotted lines to form the oval shapes within the picture.

Directions: Draw a picture of an object shaped like a oval or find a picture in a magazine and attach it to the page.

Oval

Name: _____

Directions: Trace on the dotted lines to form the triangle shapes within the picture.

Directions: Draw a picture of an object shaped like a triangle or find a picture in a magazine and attach it to the page.

Name: _____

Directions: Trace on the dotted lines to form the square shapes within the picture.

Directions: Draw a picture of an object shaped like a square or find a picture in a magazine and attach it to the page.

# Square

Name: _____

Directions: Trace on the dotted lines to form the circle shapes within the picture.

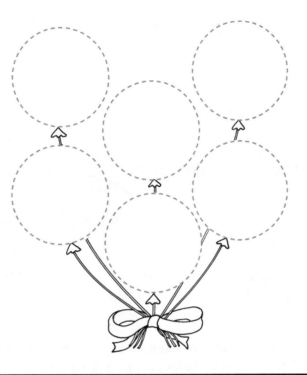

Directions: Draw a picture of an object shaped like a circle or find a picture in a magazine and attach it to the page.

# Circle

# Same and Different Activities

*Same:* items similar in appearance

*Different:* items that are not similar in appearance

The following activities will help preschoolers distinguish likenesses and differences in color, shape, size, letters, and sounds. The ability to distinguish shape, size, and pattern is a valuable prereading skill.

1. Divide your students into groups by hair color, eye color, or gender.

2. Have the students sort a collection of items by same and different color, shape and size.

3. Have students sort different styles of hats, grouping hats with the same properties together.

4. In the dramatic play area, have the students sort and match laundry items—socks, shirts, pants, dresses, and gloves.

5. Have the students taste test different foods and group them according to sweet, sour, or salty. *Safety Note:* Check for food allergies before using this activity.

6. Sort student names by first letter. Identify the different letters represented and which letter is used in the fewest and most names.

7. Create shapes using geoboards, or draw them on dry-erase boards, and ask students to re-create the shapes.

8. Have the students locate all of the letters that are the same in a writing sample. If appropriate, ask them to locate words that are the same.

9. Say two words with the same or different beginning letter sound. Use the Thumbs Up, Thumbs Down cards (page 47) and have the students respond by pointing the thumb up if both words start with the same sound. If the words start with different sounds, then the students show the thumb pointing down.

---

**Visual Discrimination Assessment: Same and Different**

Have each student group plastic shapes (plastic tangram shapes work well) by color or shape. Ask the student to explain his or her groupings.

---

# Pattern Activities

A *pattern* is a systematic way of repeating items. It is to make, do, shape, or plan an imitation of a model. Identifying and creating patterns helps children begin to break down codes in reading, math, writing, and spelling. Repetitive patterns are labeled with letters that designate how many times each symbol is repeated. For example, the pattern heart, star, heart, star would be labeled as an ABAB pattern. Each heart would be labeled with an "A" and each star would be labeled with a "B." Another type of pattern that commonly occurs is an ABB pattern. This is a pattern that uses two objects, but the second object is doubled each time (e.g., heart, star, star, heart, star, star). An ABC pattern occurs when three different objects are repeated in sequential order (e.g., heart, star, triangle, heart, star, triangle).

**Note:** Start with an easy AB pattern using two different visual props.

1. Use small paper plates with two different patterns to model how to create an alternating pattern. You may also use crayons, paper cups, wallpaper samples, napkins, or math manipulatives. Snap cubes are an excellent manipulative to use in teaching patterns. After creating simple AB patterns, ask the students to draw an example of a pattern.

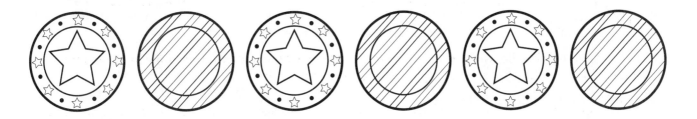

2. Have the students arrange themselves to create a boy/girl pattern. Other patterns may include sitting/standing, thumbs up/thumbs down, and wearing jeans/not wearing jeans.

3. Have the students repeat clapping patterns (after the teacher models the original pattern). Example: Teacher claps twice, pauses, and claps twice again. Students repeat the clapping pattern.

4. At snack time, encourage the students to make a pattern with two or more snack items. Let them tell you about the pattern using AB terminology.

5. Teach a song that has a repetitive pattern. The song "Head, Shoulders, Knees, and Toes" works well.

6. Use body motions to create a pattern. Ask the students to repeat the pattern. Have each student identify the kind of pattern he or she is repeating.

---

## Visual Discrimination Assessment: Patterns

Have each student demonstrate how to construct a simple AB pattern with manipulatives. Have him or her explain the reasoning behind the pattern.

---

# Sequencing Activities

Sequencing helps preschoolers recognize how events and stories occur over a period of time. Each story and event has an identifiable *beginning*, *middle*, and *end* and can be organized to retell a preschooler's favorite story or life event.

## Sequencing Cards

### Materials

- copy of Sequencing Cards (pages 97–102)
- cardstock
- 3 small resealable, plastic bags

**Preparation:** Copy the Sequencing Cards onto cardstock, laminate, and cut out the cards.

### Directions

1. Introduce the activity to the students by first asking the students to think and respond to the following questions, "What is needed to make a peanut butter and jelly sandwich? How do you make a peanut butter and jelly sandwich?"

2. Show each set of Sequencing Cards (pages 97–102) and ask the students the same questions. Allow volunteers to help organize the cards in sequential order.

**Note:** This activity may be used for independent or small group instruction during center time.

## Additional Sequencing Activities

1. Tell the students, "When we line up, we are using numbers to create order. We have a student in first place, a student in second, and a student in third." Play this game each day and, if appropriate, have the daily helper be first. Ask the daily helper to pick who will be second. Ask the second person to pick the third person. This game may also be used to illustrate the concept of first, middle, and last using a group of objects.

2. Sequence the life cycles of a monarch butterfly, a chicken, or a frog. Set up a science center to hatch classroom butterflies, chickens, or frogs. Introduce the students to books that outline the individual life cycles and unique vocabulary associated with the process. Sequencing picture cards may be created to allow the students to track the life cycle changes at the science center.

3. Cooking activities are a great way to help students understand the concept of completing work in a sequence. (i.e., To make a cake, you turn on the oven, mix the batter, etc.)

4. Give each child three-step directions and ask the child to do them in the correct sequence. Example: Stand up, walk to the door, and open the door. Limit the number of steps to three until students are comfortable with the concept.

---

**Visual Discrimination Assessment: Sequencing**

For a Visual Discrimination Assessment, have the students arrange sets of Sequencing Cards in order or redraw a 3–4 picture sequence of an everyday activity (e.g., getting ready for school, cleaning a bedroom, making breakfast).

---

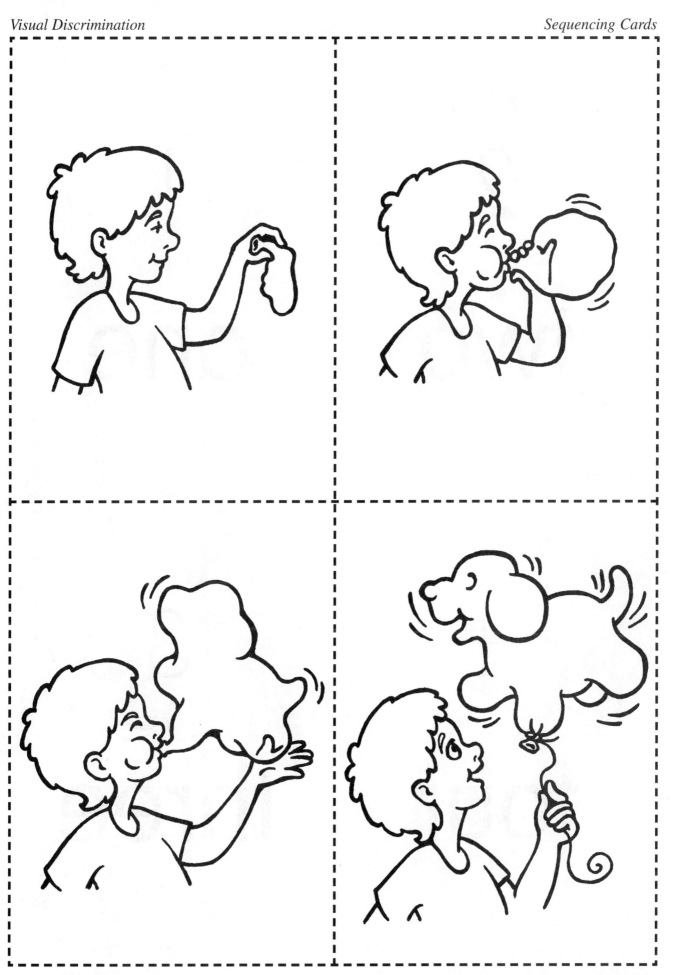

2

two

1

one

4

four

3

three

98

2

two

1

one

4

four

3

three

2

two

1

one

4

four

3

three

# Concepts of Print Activities

*Print* carries a message. It tells us what an author is trying to tell the reader. The print is read and understood by everyone and carries a message to all readers. *Concepts of print* include proper book handling, left-to-right reading directionality, and the differences among letters, words, and sentences. *Directionality* is the orderly manner in which letters, sounds, words, and sentences are written and read to deliver a message to the reader. In the English language, directionality refers to reading of text on a page from left to right and top to bottom.

1. Using word cards on a pocket chart, model how to form a sentence beginning at the top-left corner of the pocket chart. Read from left to right.

2. Name the letters contained in each word as you write them on the board. Say each word once all letters have been written (e.g., *t, o, d, a, y—today*).

3. Model left-to-right directionality by asking a student to point to the place where the class should begin reading words in a big book.

4. Model one-to-one word correspondence while the class reads a daily message aloud. Enhance this activity by writing the words of the daily message on individual index cards and working with the students to create the daily message on the carpet. This is a great way to emphasize uppercase letters at the beginning of a sentence and periods and question marks at the end of a sentence. The students will also practice print directionality as they reconstruct the sentence.

## Concepts of Print Assessment

A Concepts of Print Assessment is included on page 130. The checklist covers the following areas: directionality, letters and words, grammatical conventions, and meaning.

# Concepts of Print Activities *(cont.)*

Preschoolers can learn proper directionality from a teacher modeling how to read during storytime. Preschoolers easily point to the words from left to right as they pretend to read. These activities will help preschoolers master directionality and build their confidence in their ability to read.

1. Hold a storybook by the spine and hand it to a student, asking him or her to show you the front of the book or the back of the book.

2. Identify the author and illustrator of the book and where this information may be found on the title page in a book. Explain that the *author* is the person who wrote the book and the *illustrator* is the person who drew the pictures.

3. Read one or more sentences on the page while pointing to each word, stopping at the end of a line of text on the right-hand side of the page. Have a student demonstrate the return sweep by moving his or her finger from the right-hand side of the page to the left-hand side in order to begin reading a new sentence.

4. Read a familiar story backward. Open the book's back page and begin reading the end of the story first. Watch the students to see their reactions. Ask the students, "Does the story makes sense? Why is the story not making sense? Where should we begin reading the story?"

5. While you point to the words, switch the line order within a story and read the second sentence first and the first sentence second. Ask the students, "Do the sentences make sense? What was wrong with the way we were reading?"

## Directionality Sorting Cards

1. Use the Directionality Cards (pages 105–124). Copy the cards onto cardstock and laminate them.

2. Sort the picture cards into groups, illustrating the spatial concepts: top, bottom, over, under, front, back, inside, outside, up, and down.

3. Introduce two directional concepts at a time to help the students learn directional terms at a reasonable pace (i.e., begin with top and bottom, followed later by up and down). Continue to add new terms as students indicate readiness.

# Letter and Word Activities

*Letters* or *graphemes* are the symbolic representations of sounds used to make up a word. Young preschoolers still have difficulty distinguishing individual letters from a word. The following activities will help the students learn the individual letters and how letters are put together to create words.

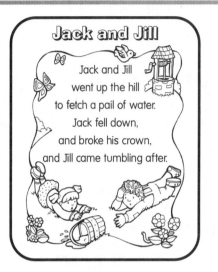

1. Ask individual students to point to words in a song, rhyme, or poem written on chart paper to demonstrate word-by-word matching. This is an excellent time to introduce what a *space* is. Follow the activity directions on page 126 and have students create a Space Creature using a craft stick. Once completed, the students can be called up in front of the class to use the Space Creature to mark a space between words in a sentence.

2. Ask individual students to count words in a group of sentences. Direct the students to identify which sentence has the most and fewest words.

3. Ask the students to point to the first and last letters within a word, the first and last words in a sentence, and the punctuation marks.

4. Model writing a sentence on the chalkboard. Talk about why we use uppercase letters to mark the beginning of a sentence.

5. Ask individual students to underline the "letter of the week" contained within the daily message (e.g., the letter of the week is *Yy*—underline each *Yy* found within the words that make up the daily message).

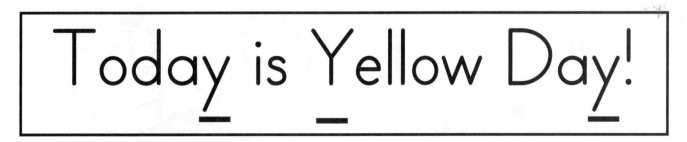

# Space Creature

## Materials

- copy of Space Creature (below) for each student
- craft stick for each student
- craft glue
- scissors

## Directions

1. Give each student a copy of the Space Creature and have him or her cut it out.

2. Demonstrate how to apply the proper amount of glue to the craft stick.

3. Have the student place the cutout on top of the glue.

4. Set the sticks aside and allow time to dry.

- - - - - - - - - - - - - - - - - - - - - - - - - - - - - - - - - - - - - -

# Flannel Board, Puppet, and Drama Activities

*Print* carries a message. It tells us what an author is trying to tell the reader in a certain language. Flannel board, puppet, and drama activities help students retell a story from beginning to end, demonstrating their grasp of the printed materials shared with them.

## Flannel Board Activities

1. Incorporate a flannel board into your library center. Select storybooks with matching flannel storyboard kits to read to the class. Demonstrate how the students can use the flannel board and commercial (or homemade) storyboard kits to re-enact the story in their own words.

2. Introduce new vocabulary the students will encounter during storytime and define the terms for them. Explain that the *setting* of the story is where the story takes place. Show the students the house pattern (page 128). In the story, "The Three Bears," the house represents the setting.

   Pull out the flannel board *characters* (page 129) and explain that characters are the people in a story— Goldilocks, Papa Bear, Mama Bear, and Baby Bear. Explain that the way in which the problem is solved within the story is known as the *plot*. For the plot, use the following patterns (page 128): bowl of porridge, broken chair, and broken bed with the character patterns to act out the story.

## Puppet Activities

1. Puppets are a great way to teach difficult concepts to preschoolers. Purchase commercial puppets (or make simple puppets from socks and paper bags). Use them during reading time. Give each puppet an identity: a unique personality, distinctive appearance, and voice. Have the puppet ask the students questions about the book while reviewing some of the basic concepts of print. Have the puppet ask the students questions about the book while reviewing some of the basic concepts of print (e.g., In the story, "The Three Little Pigs," the puppet can ask which pig is the smartest and why.).

2. Provide students with paper plates, bags, socks, craft remnants, and glue. Allow them to create their own puppets. Separate your students into different groups and direct them to use their puppets to re-enact a story.

## Drama Activities

1. Assign students different parts of a book and ask the students to re-enact the story.

2. Help students re-create a setting from a favorite book in the dramatic play area or block area using paper, boxes, and craft remnants (e.g., create Cinderella's castle or a post office).

# Three Bears Patterns

house

porridge

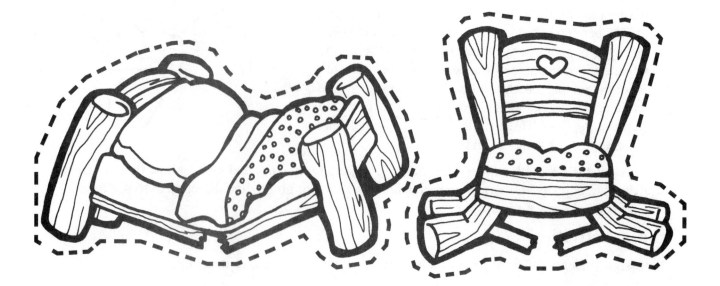

**bed**                                              **chair**

# Three Bears Patterns *(cont.)*

**Papa Bear**

**Mama Bear**

**Goldilocks**

**Baby Bear**

# Concepts of Print Assessment

**Name** _____ **Date** _____

## Directionality

1. Holds the book correctly

2. Identifies the front and the back of book

3. Points to the first and the last word in book

4. Starts with the left page before the right

5. Goes from left to right

6. Makes return sweep

## Letters and Words

1. Performs word-by-word matching

2. Recognizes different letters

3. Recognizes different words

4. Identifies first and last letter of words

## Grammatical Conventions

1. Recognizes full stop (period)

2. Recognizes question mark

3. Points to uppercase letters

## Print Conveys a Message

1. Explains what book is about

**Comments**

# Alphabet Activities

The *alphabet* consists of a set of 26 symbols known as letters. Most educators teach letter recognition and letter sounds (phonics) simultaneously.

1. Begin an alphabet lesson with singing or reciting the alphabet. Write the Alphabet Songs (page 133) on chart paper to display for the students.

2. As the songs become more familiar, the teacher should point to visuals such as the Alphabet Cards (page 134–138). Then the students should begin to recognize those squiggles as the letters they are singing. If at all possible, each child should have a set of Alphabet Cards to put in sequential order.

3. Use a sand or rice table to draw letters.

4. Finger-paint letters.

5. Fill a small, resealable plastic bag with colored hand gel or finger paint and allow students to draw letters on the bags with their fingers.

6. Use magnetic letters on cookie sheets or on magnetic boards.

7. Make a snake shape using play dough. Then use the dough to form different letters.

8. Have the students write the letters on dry-erase boards. If you cannot afford to purchase individual boards, salt trays may be used for individual boards.

9. Find letters in magazines or newspapers. Cut them out and make a collage.

10. Locate letters in school environmental print such as the exit sign, the name of the school, the restrooms, and the library.

11. Introduce your students to the different ways letters are formed. For example, show the students how the letter *a* may be formed differently, but it is still called an *a.* Pick a letter of the alphabet and show it in a variety of books. Cut out the font examples. Make a collage for each letter.

12. Use the Letter Practice Sheets (pages 152–177) to practice forming each uppercase and lowercase letter. Space is provided on each page for students to draw additional pictures beginning with the featured letter.

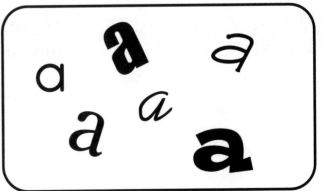

# Alphabet Activities *(cont.)*

12. Make two sets of the Alphabet Cards (pages 134–138). Initially, give students 10 cards with letters previously studied. Create an uppercase and lowercase matching game by cutting each card in half. Students may use the second set to practice letter recognition.

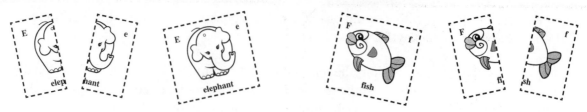

13. Give students the opportunity to write the letters of the alphabet, first using unlined paper. Move on to lined paper as each student becomes developmentally ready.

14. Using pages 139–151, have students practice identifying uppercase and lowercase letters. You may wish to have them circle uppercase letters with one color crayon and lower case letters with another color.

15. Using pages 152–177, have students practice writing letters. They may color the picture on the page and then draw a picture starting with the featured letter. Or the students may find a magazine picture that starts with the featured letter and glue it on the page.

16. Introduce multisensory activities to the art center and outdoor playtime by using the Multisensory and Movement Activities (pages 178–179).

---

### Alphabet Assessment

For an Alphabet Assessment, use the Alphabet Cards on pages 134–138. Copy the cards onto cardstock, laminate, and cut each card vertically in half so that there is an uppercase part and a lowercase part. Mix up the cards so they are not in alphabetical order. Then have the student identify each letter.

---

# Alphabet Songs

Often students do not distinctly sing the individual letters l, m, n, o, and p in the traditional version of the alphabet song. The song below teaches the students to separate each letter.

The ABC's

a b c d
e f g
h i j k
l m n
o p q
r s t
u v w
x y z

Now we know the al-pha-bet.
Next time we will be all set!

*Sing to the tune of
"Twinkle, Twinkle Little Star"*

The Backward Song

Z Y X W V U T

S R Q P

O N M L K

J I H  G F E

D C B and A.

Now we know our ZYX's
Next time we will go to Texas.

*Sing to the tune of
"The Alphabet Song"*

# Alphabet Cards

A    a

**apple**

B    b

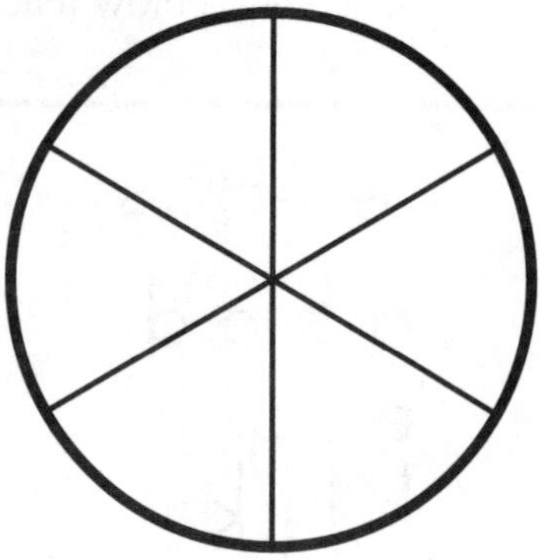

**ball**

C    c

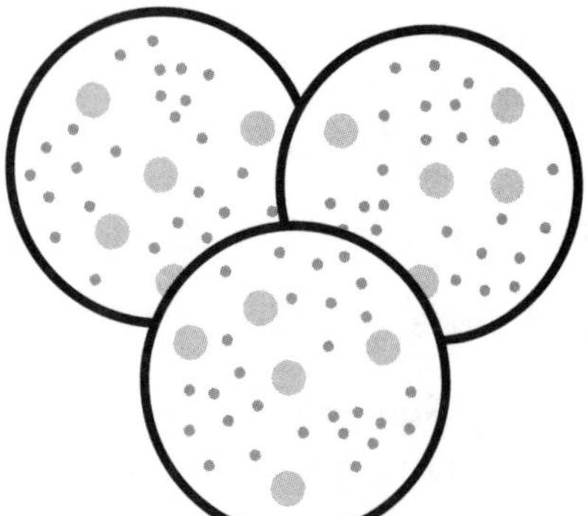

**cookies**

D    d

**dinosaur**

E    e

**elephant**

F    f

**fish**

134

# Alphabet Cards *(cont.)*

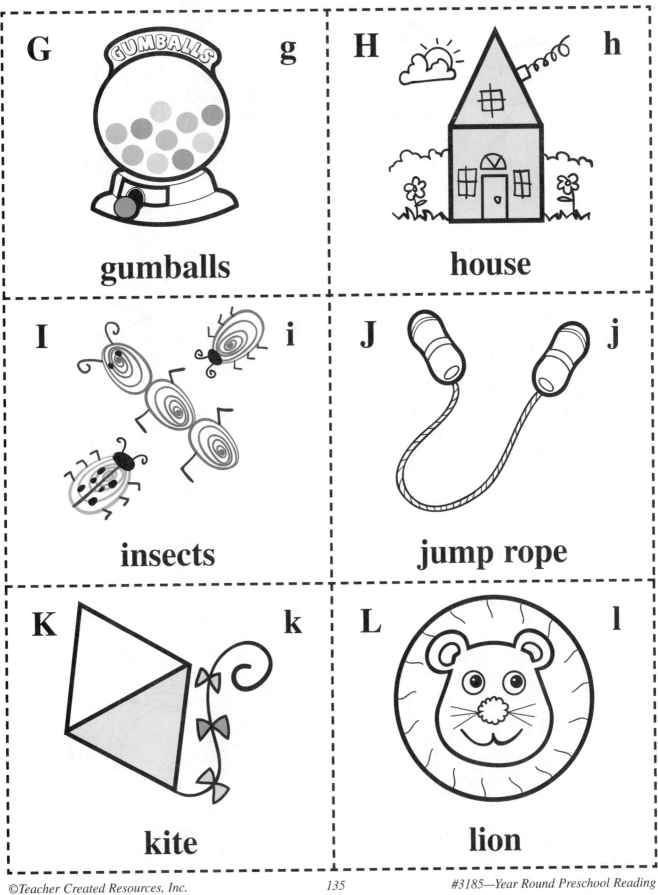

G g
**gumballs**

H h
**house**

I i
**insects**

J j
**jump rope**

K k
**kite**

L l
**lion**

# Alphabet Cards *(cont.)*

**M**     **m**

**mittens**

**N**     **n**

**newspaper**

**O**     **o**

**octopus**

**P**     **p**

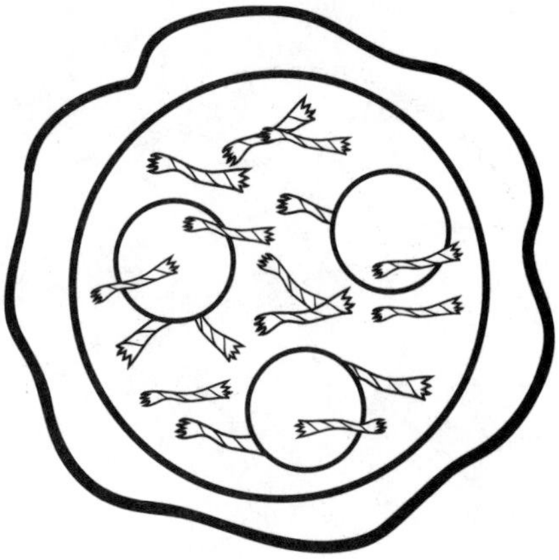

**pizza**

**Q**     **q**

**quilt**

**R**     **r**

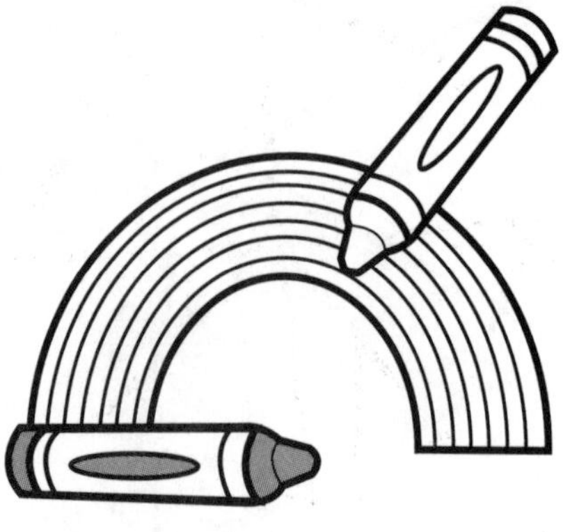

**rainbow**

# Alphabet Cards *(cont.)*

**S** 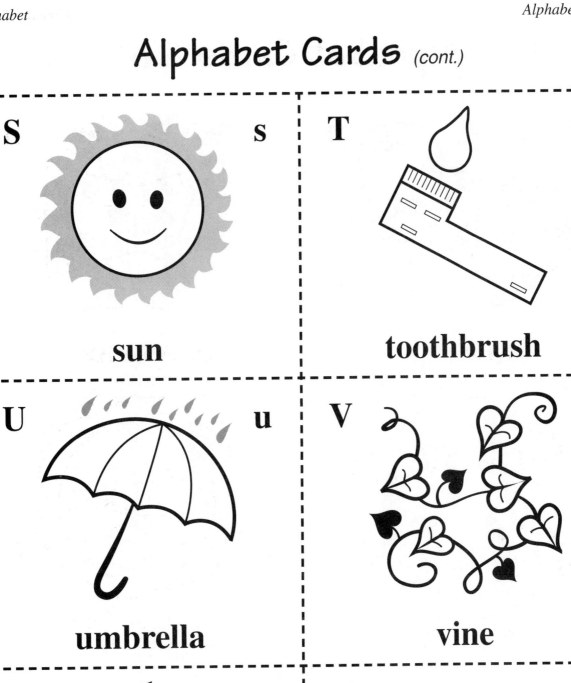 **s**

**sun**

**T** **t**

**toothbrush**

**U** **u**

**umbrella**

**V** **v**

**vine**

**W** 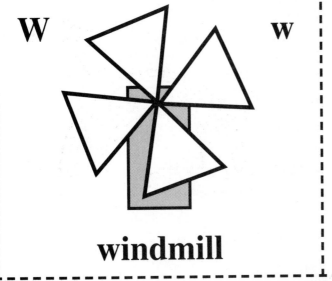 **w**

**windmill**

**X** 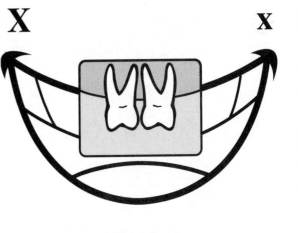 **x**

**x-ray**

# Alphabet Cards (cont.)

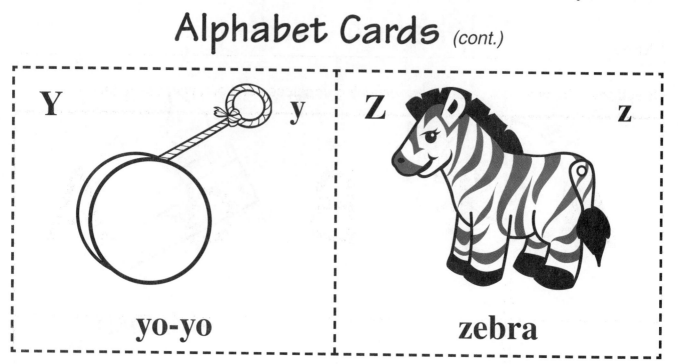

Y / y
**yo-yo**

Z / z
**zebra**

Name _____

**Directions:** Draw a circle around the matching uppercase and/or lowercase letter.

| A | F | B | a | A |
|---|---|---|---|---|
| B | b | X | B | D |
| C | o | C | c | Q |
| D | O | g | D | d |

Name _____

**Directions:** Draw a circle around the matching uppercase and/or lowercase letter.

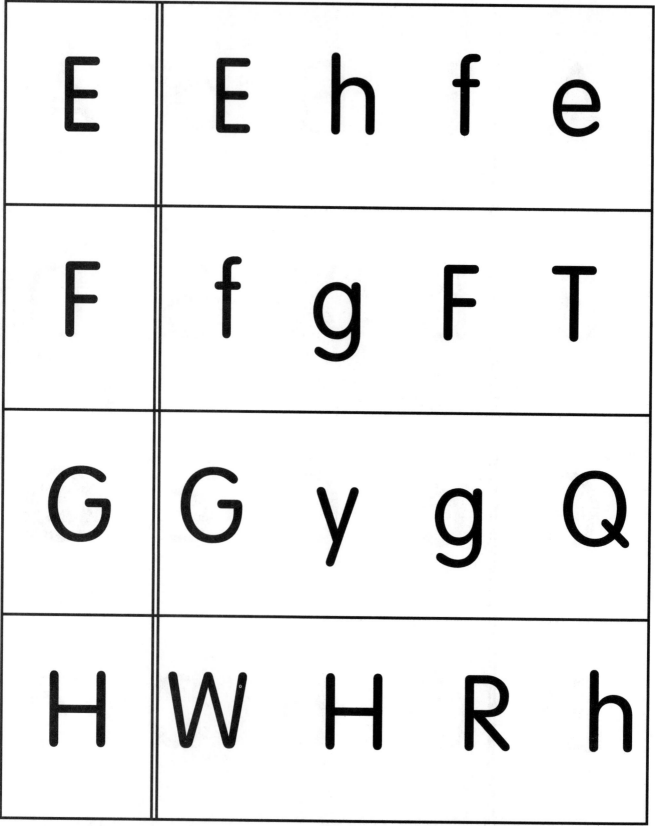

| E | E   h   f   e |
|---|---------------|
| F | f   g   F   T |
| G | G   y   g   Q |
| H | W   H   R   h |

Name _____

**Directions:** Draw a circle around the matching uppercase and/or lowercase letter.

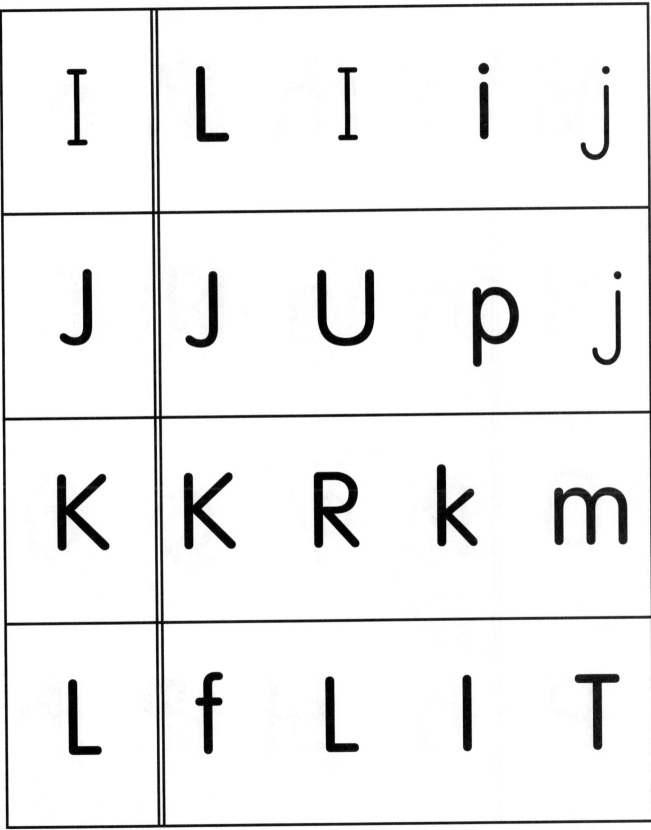

Name _____

**Directions:** Draw a circle around the matching uppercase and/or lowercase letter.

| M | n m M N |
|---|---------|
| N | n W N m |
| O | P q O o |
| P | b p R P |

142

Name _____

**Directions:** Draw a circle around the matching uppercase and/or lowercase letter.

| Q | g    q    G    Q |
|---|------------------|
| R | r    B    R    s |
| S | m    s    S    W |
| T | T    I    f    t |

Name _____

**Directions:** Draw a circle around the matching uppercase and/or lowercase letter.

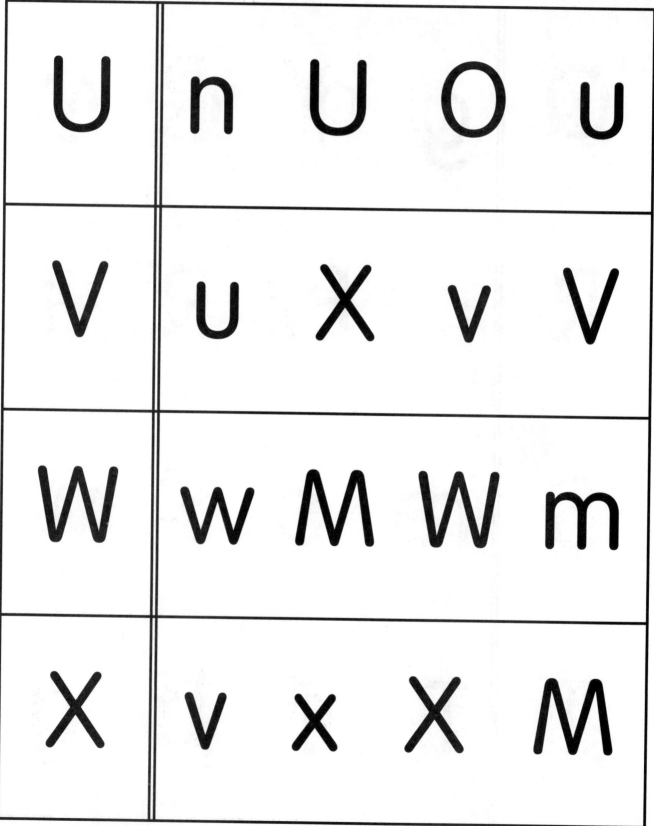

| U | n U O u |
|---|---|
| V | u X v V |
| W | w M W m |
| X | v x X M |

Name _____

**Directions:** Draw a circle around the matching uppercase and/or lowercase letter.

| Y | g Y R y |
|---|---------|
| Z | m z Z l |
| a | e a A t |
| b | B d b g |

Name _____

**Directions:** Draw a circle around the matching uppercase and/or lowercase letter.

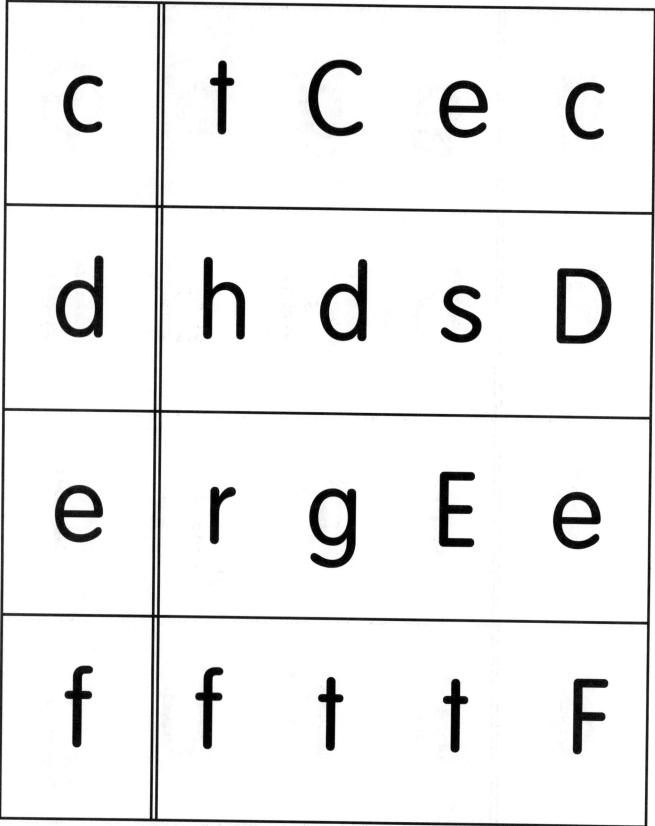

| c | t C e c |
|---|---------|
| d | h d s D |
| e | r g E e |
| f | f t t F |

Name _____

**Directions:** Draw a circle around the matching uppercase and/or lowercase letter.

| g | e g o G |
|---|---------|
| h | b H d h |
| i | i I j l |
| J | i I J j |

Name _____

**Directions:** Draw a circle around the matching uppercase and/or lowercase letter.

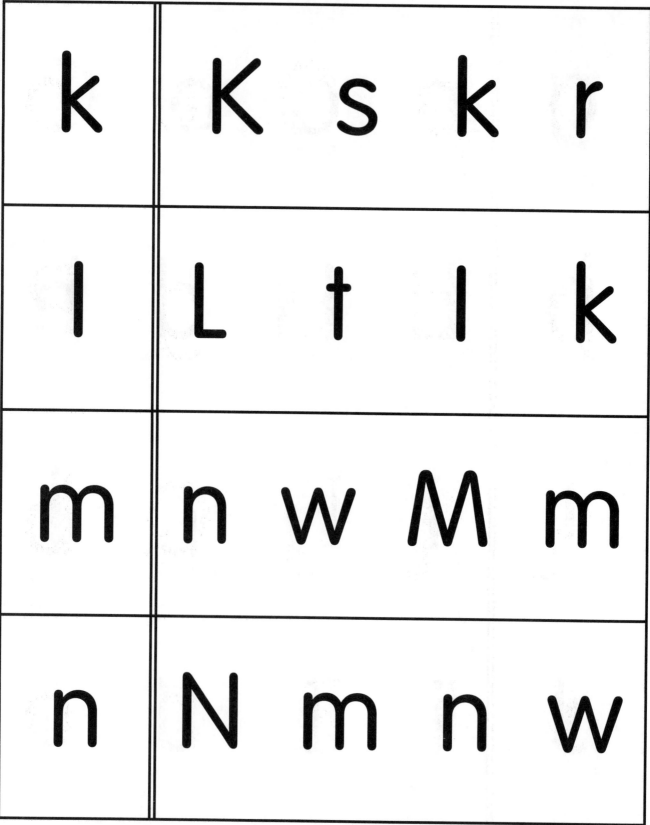

| k | K   s   k   r |
|---|---------------|
| l | L   t   l   k |
| m | n   w   M   m |
| n | N   m   n   w |

148

Name _____

**Directions:** Draw a circle around the matching uppercase and/or lowercase letter.

| o | p | O | U | o |
|---|---|---|---|---|
| p | d | p | g | P |
| q | q | g | Q | b |
| r | t | R | r | o |

Name _____

**Directions:** Draw a circle around the matching uppercase and/or lowercase letter.

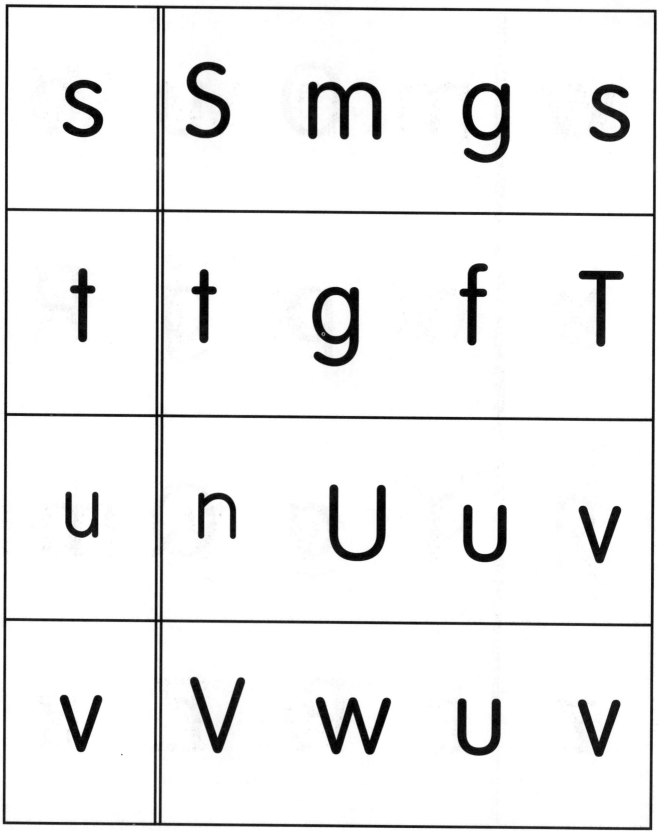

Name _____

**Directions:** Draw a circle around the matching uppercase and/or lowercase letter.

| w | m  n  w  W |
|---|---|
| x | m  x  f  X |
| y | Y  v  y  m |
| z | z  w  Z  x |

Name

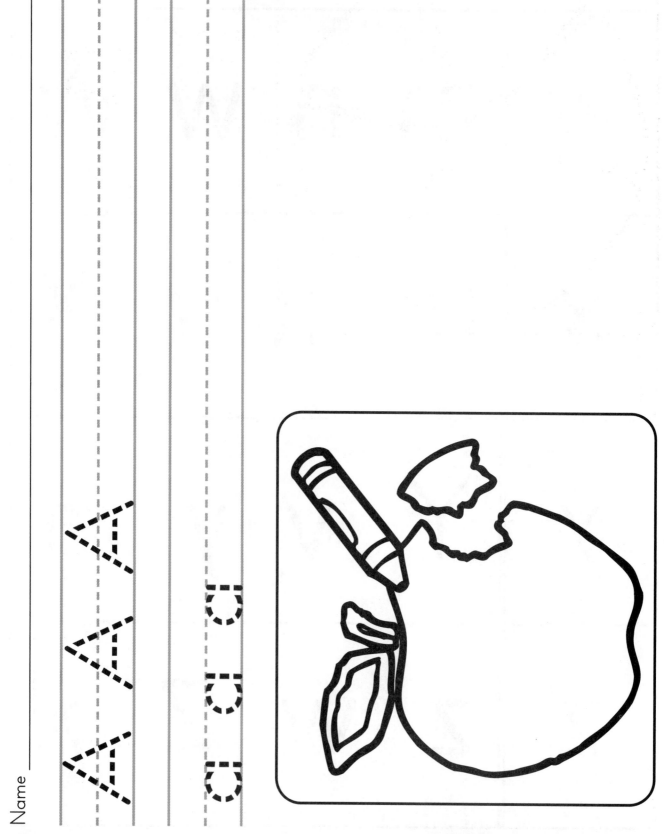

Name

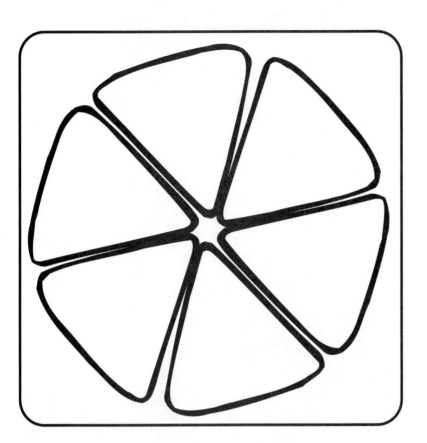

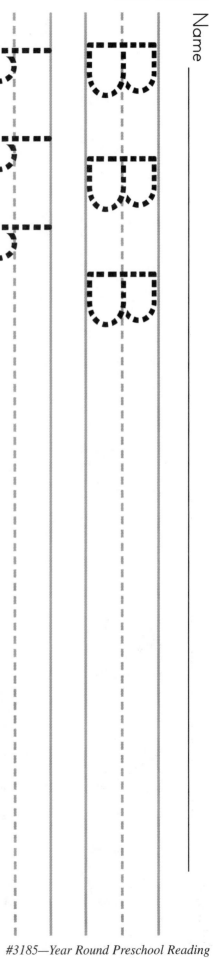

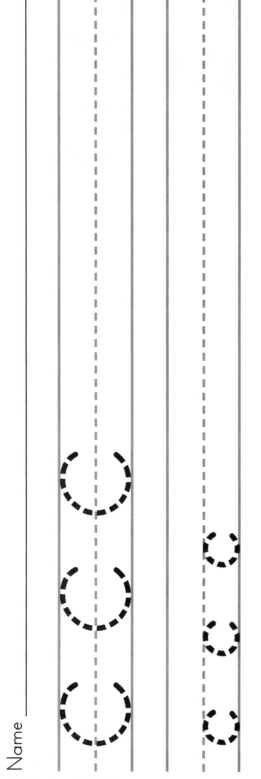

Name

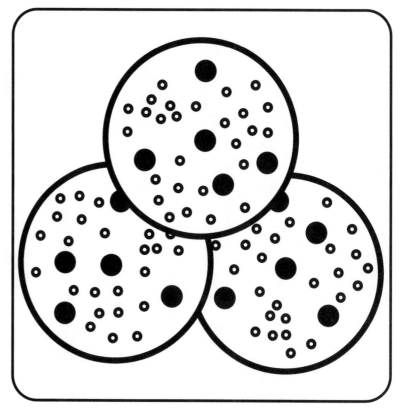

Name

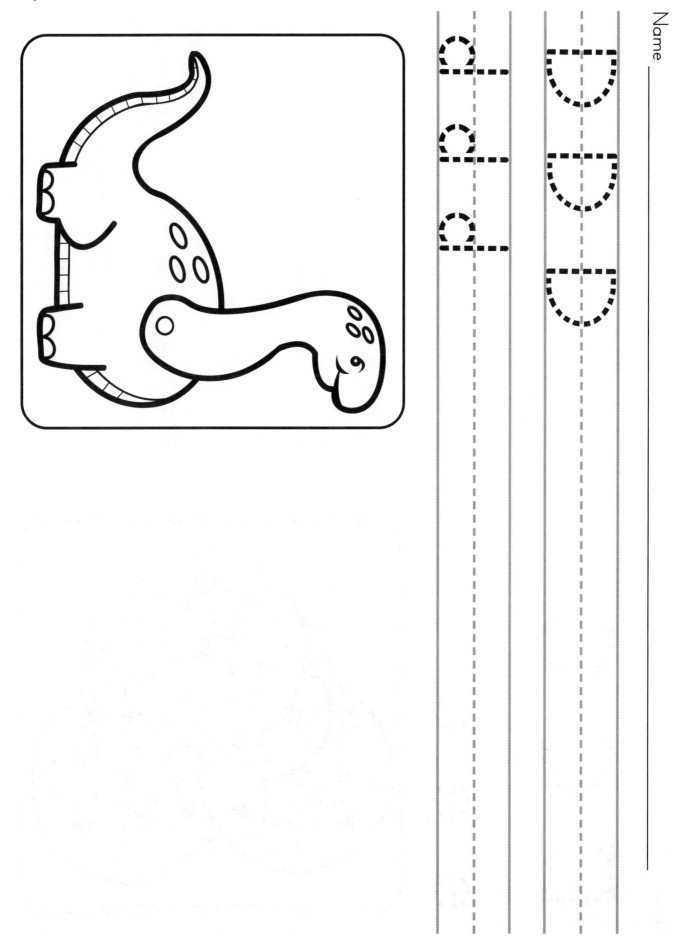

Name

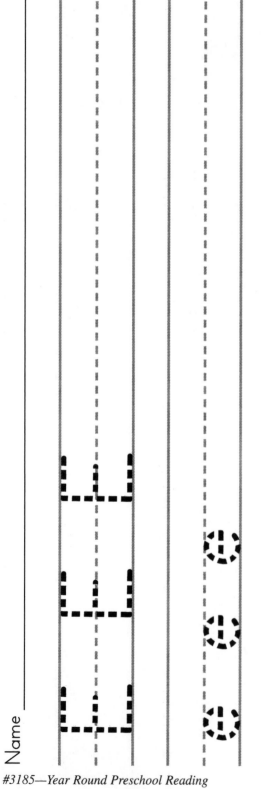

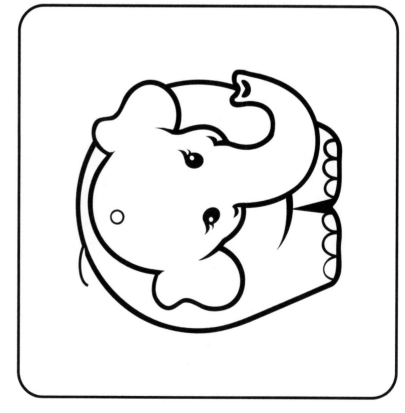

Name

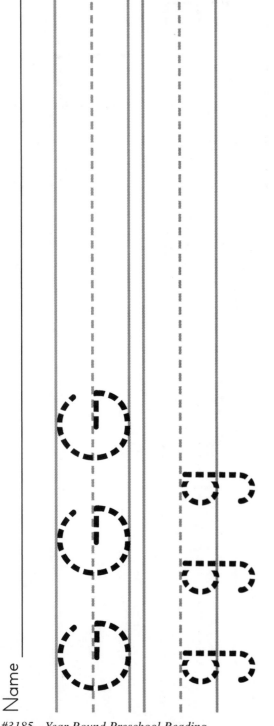

Name

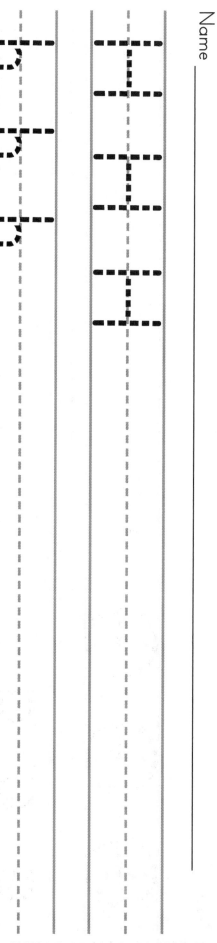

Name

Name

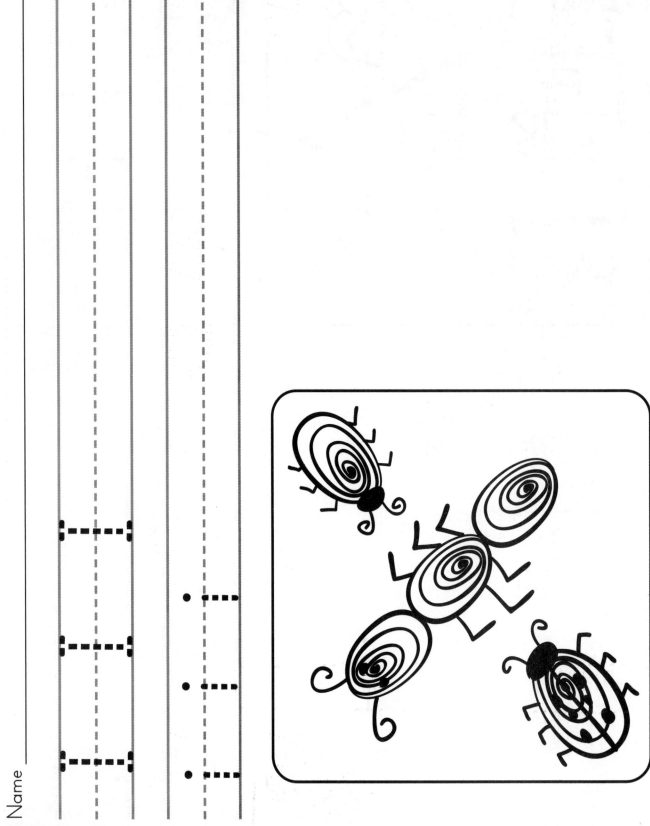

Name

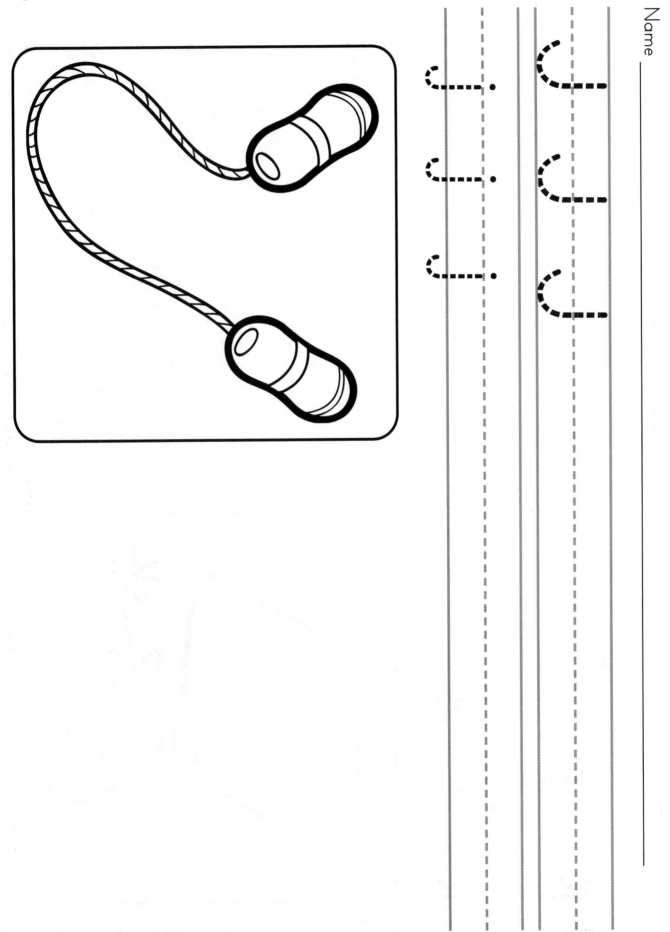

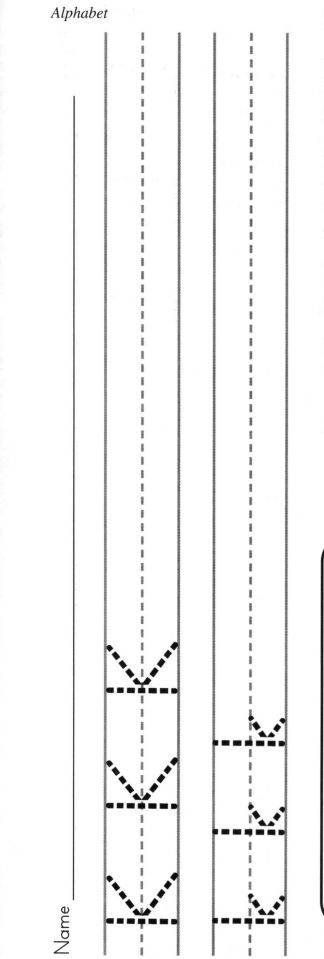

Name

162

Name

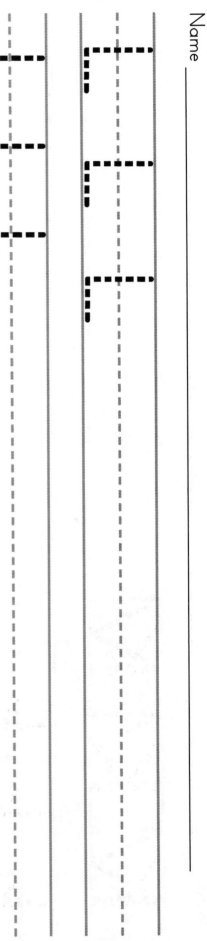

Name

Name

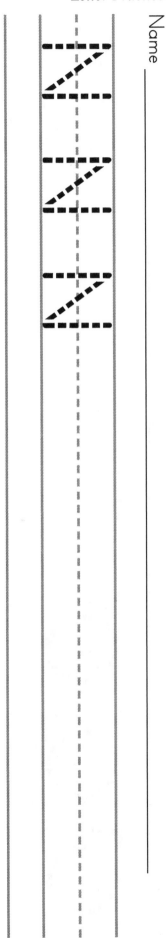

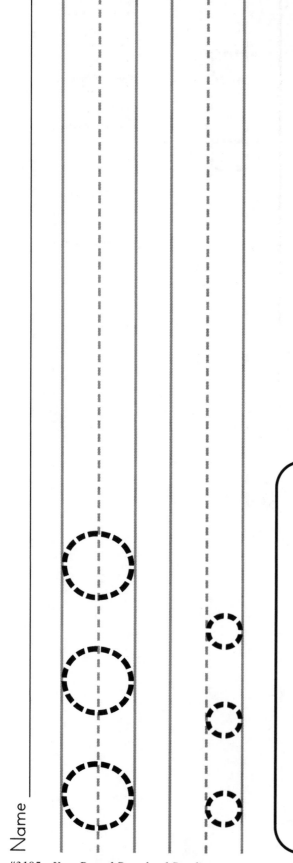

Name

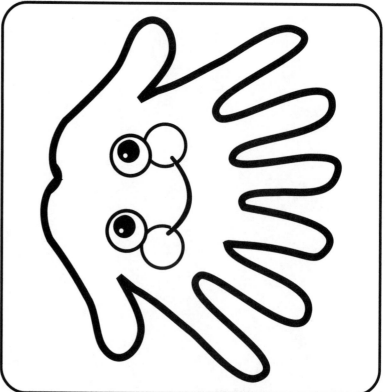

*Letter Practice*

Name

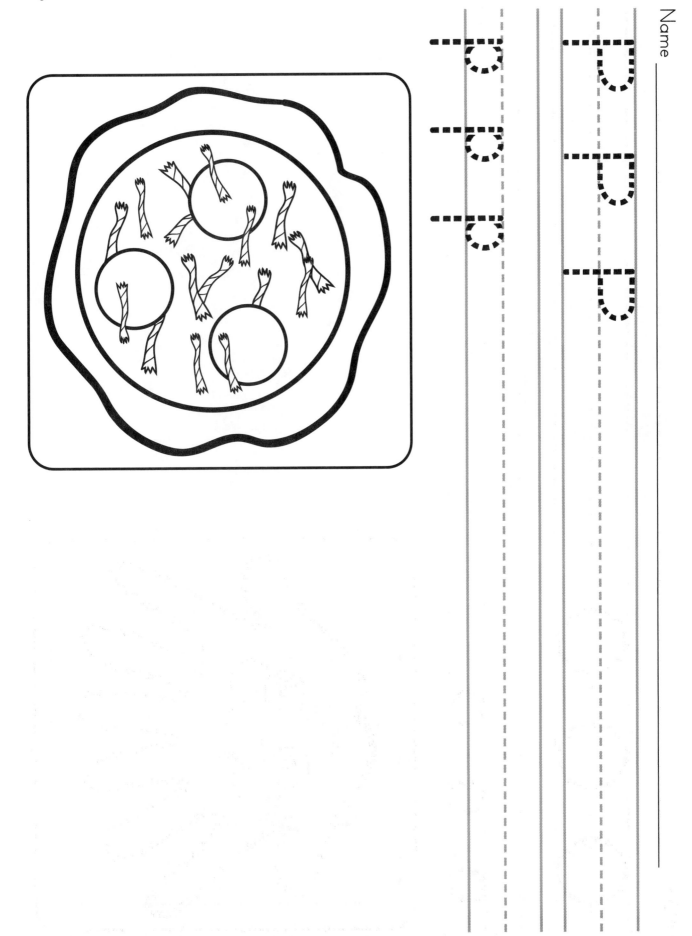

Name

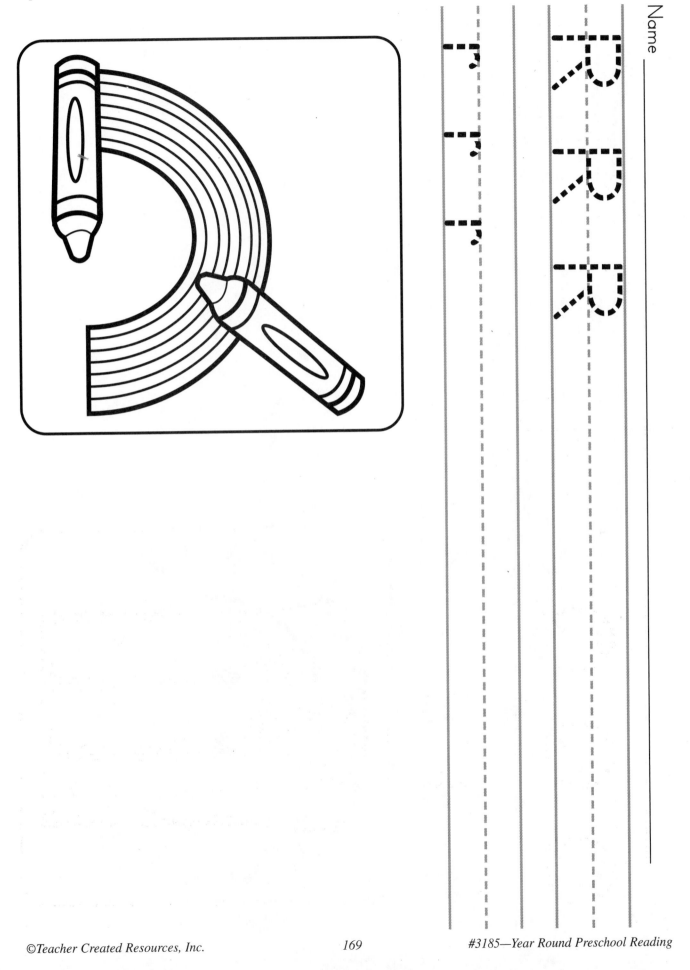

Name

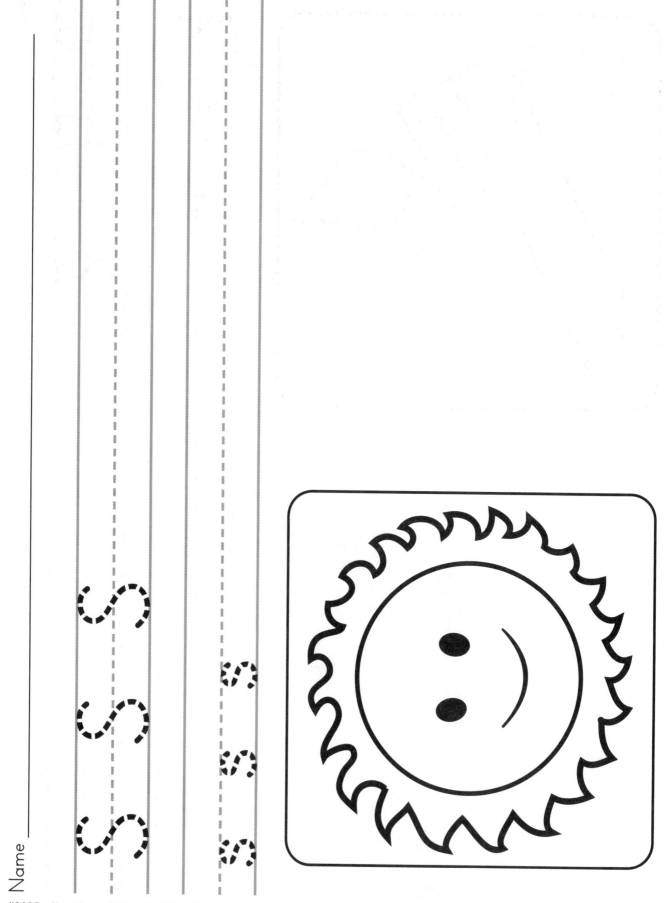

Name

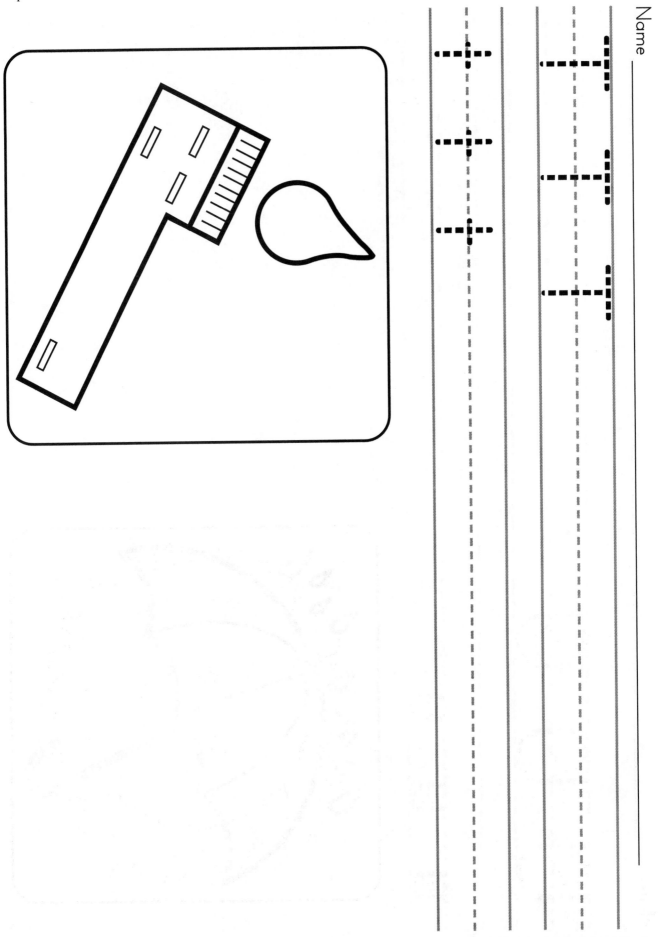

Name

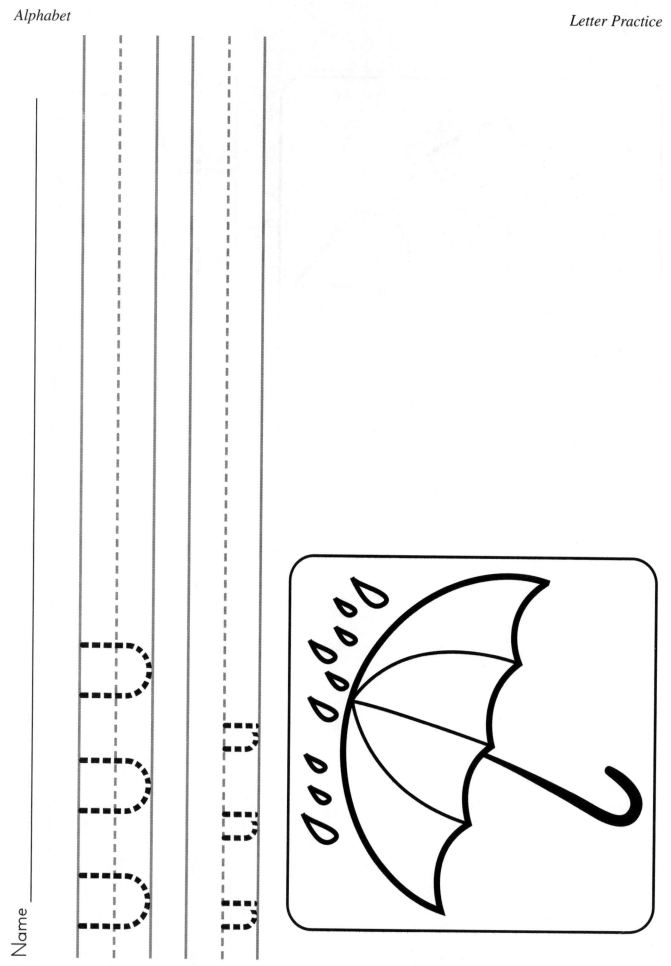

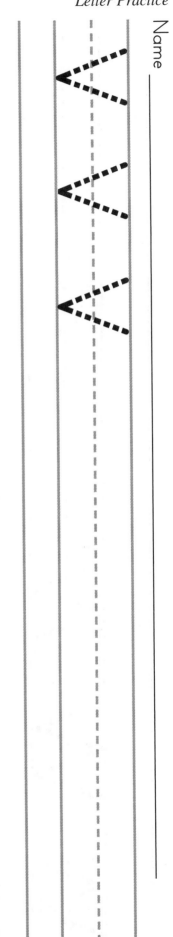

Name

Name

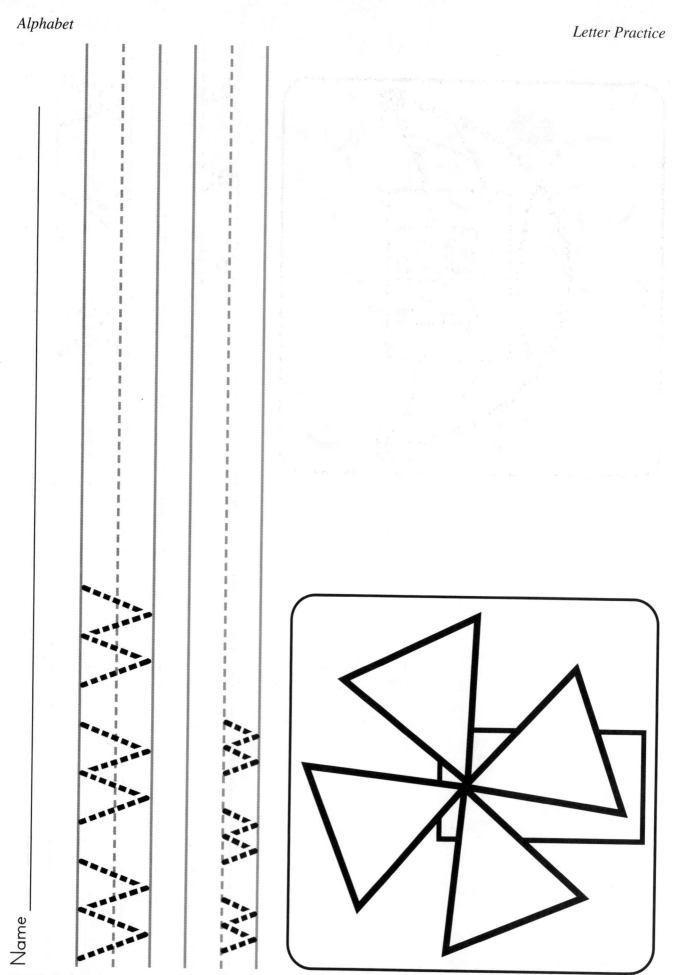

Name

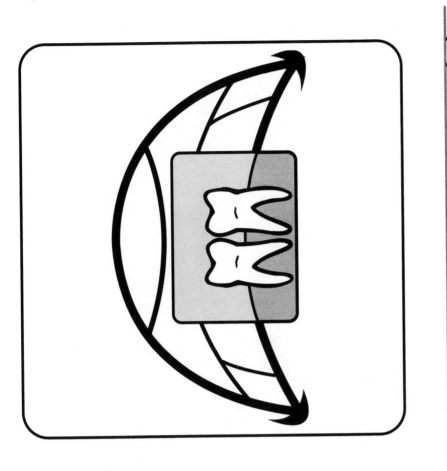

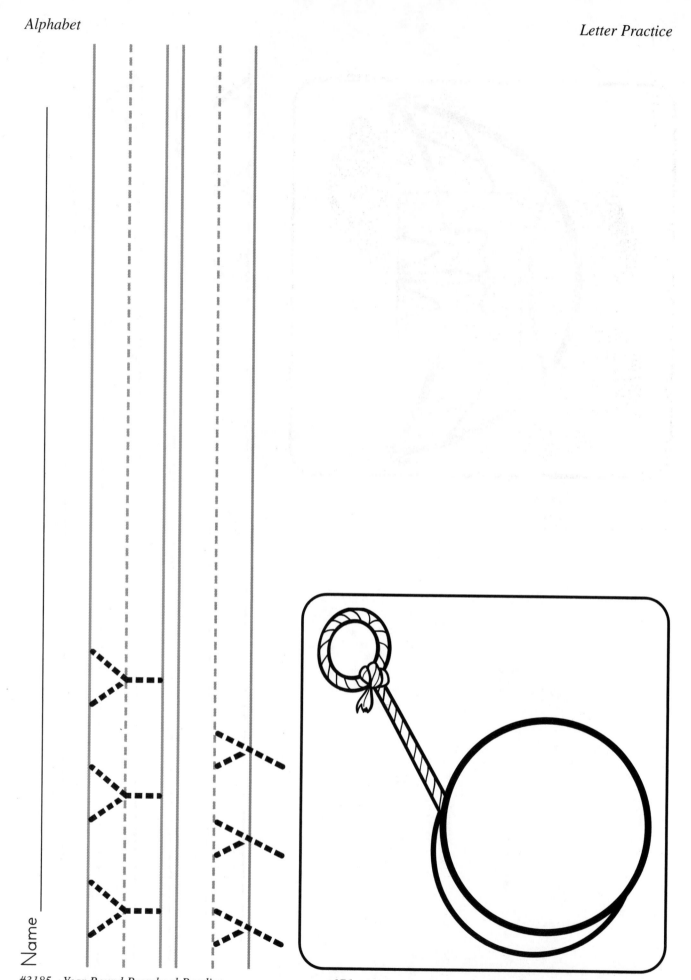

Name

Name

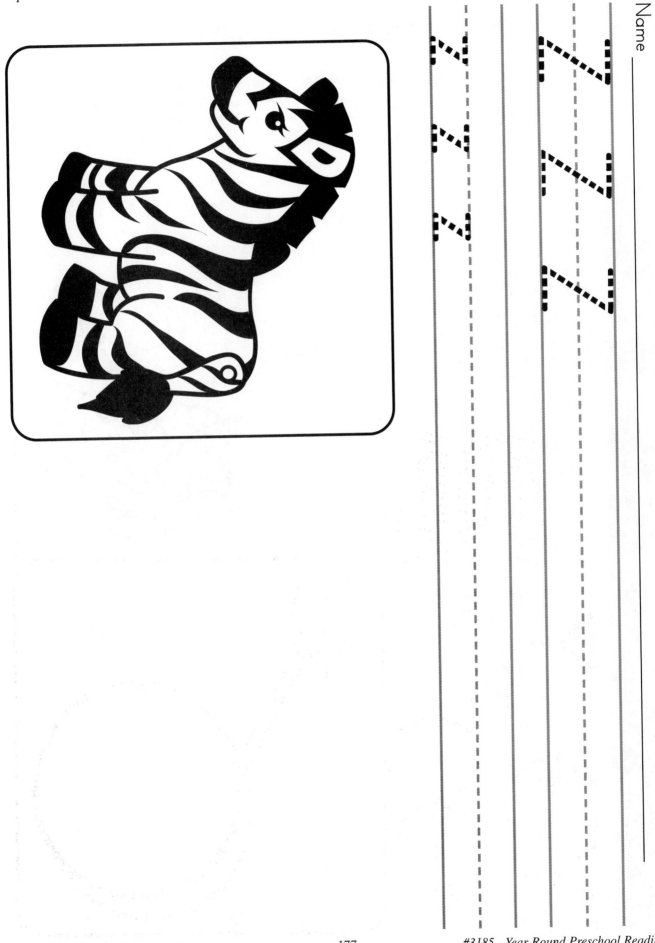

177

# Multisensory Activities

Have the students write the featured letter on a whole sheet of paper. Provide a variety of materials for students to glue on top of a letter outline. You may use accessible objects such as beans, macaroni, or rice, or you may want to use objects that correspond to the featured alphabet letter. Some items, such as pudding, can be used directly on the letters. Other items will need to be glued onto the letters. Choose from the following objects:

**A** acorns, apple stickers

**B** beans, bird seed, buttons, bow-tie pasta, brads, burlap

**C** candy, cotton balls, corn kernels, crayons (broken), cereal, candles, confetti, caps, corks

**D** dots, dough

**E** erasers, egg shells

**F** flour, feathers, felt, fabric, fuzz, fur, flower petals

**G** glitter, granola, glue (colored), gauze

**H** hole punches, heart punches

**I** ink, icing

**J** jellybeans, junk, jewelry, pieces of jump rope

**K** kidney beans

**L** leaves, licorice, lace, lima beans

**M** magazine pages, macaroni

**N** newspaper, nuts, noodles, netting

**O** oats, o-shaped cereal, orange ovals (cut outs)

**P** packing peanuts, peanuts, paper curls, pipe cleaners, pasta, popcorn, peas (dried), paper clips

**Q** Q-tips®, "quicksand" (heavy, wet sand)

**R** rice, raisins, ribbon, red rectangles, rope

**S** sand, seeds, sequins, pieces of sponge, salt, sticks, sugar (colored), spaghetti

**T** toothpicks, tube noodles, twigs, tapioca

**U** umbrellas (miniature)

**V** velvet, vanilla pudding, Velcro®

**W** white tissue, wiggle eyes, wood chips

**X** cardboard box pieces, floor tile separators (hardware store)

**Y** yellow yarn

**Z** zigzags (rick-rack fabric trim), zippers

# Movement Activities

Reinforce sounds by having students participate in movement activities that correspond to each letter of the alphabet. One approach is to have students participate in a variety of movement activities for each letter of the alphabet. Another approach is to select only one movement activity for each letter of the alphabet. Once practiced, students will associate the movement with the sound and letter of the alphabet. Then, turn the movement activity into a game by displaying a letter of the alphabet. See pages 134–138 for alphabet card patterns. The cards can be enlarged as needed. Students must perform the movement activity that corresponds to the displayed letter. Continue displaying other alphabet cards. Students must change their movement to match the letter being displayed. Pretend to. . .

| | |
|---|---|
| A | fly like an airplane, walk like an alligator |
| B | fly like a butterfly, blow bubbles, bounce a ball |
| C | crawl like a crocodile, crab walk |
| D | dance, dig, beat a drum |
| E | walk like an elephant, move like a train engine |
| F | go fishing, fly, leap like a frog, freeze |
| G | gallop, grow like a plant |
| H | hop like a bunny, play hopscotch |
| I | move like an inchworm, scratch an itch |
| J | jump, juggle, jump rope |
| K | kick, hop like a kangaroo, fly a kite |
| L | leap, climb a ladder |
| M | march, act like a monkey |
| N | hammer nails, read the newspaper, nap |
| O | wiggle arms like an octopus |
| P | punch, pop like popcorn, put together a puzzle |
| Q | quack like a duck, quiver, be completely quiet |
| R | roll, read, rub your arm |
| S | spread, sneak around, slither like a snake, cut with scissors |
| T | trot, brush teeth, hit a tennis ball |
| U | put up an umbrella |
| V | play volleyball |
| W | wave, wiggle, wheelbarrow walk, act like windshield wipers, wash the car |
| X | cross arms like an X, use fingers to make Xs in the air |
| Y | play with a yo-yo, eat yogurt |
| Z | zip a zipper, act like an animal from the zoo |

# Phonics Activities

*Phonics* refers to relationship between the letters of written language and the sounds of spoken language. It includes breaking apart and manipulating the sounds in words represented by sounds in the letters of the alphabet. The letters are then blended together to form words. Students will quickly master the letter-sound relationships through these fun, hands-on activities.

1. Commercial letter tubs may be purchased. However, teachers can create their own letter containers by collecting small objects (one object per student) that begin with the letter sounds in the alphabet. Bags or small, clear plastic containers can be labeled for easy storage and retrieval. Every time you introduce a letter, empty the contents of the container and explain how they relate to the letter (e.g., *ball* begins with /b/, *bat* begins with /b/). Select two or three letters previously studied. Empty the containers. Ask the students to sort each item into the correct container according to its beginning sound.

2. Make collages using magazine pictures of objects beginning with the featured letter sound. Ask each student to share his or her page with the class. Collect all the pages and staple them together to create a class letter book. This is an excellent activity for the home-school connection.

3. Do a Letter Find in the classroom. Show an Alphabet Card (pages 134–138) and say the sound. Ask the students to find something in the room that starts with that sound. For example: /b/(board), /t/(television), /w/(window), /p/(pencil), and /d/(door).

4. Make a class alphabet book. Take photos of students holding objects that begin with the featured letter. If taking photos is not an option, use student-drawn pictures.

5. Sing a song using the consonant letter sounds to the tune of the theme from Batman "BBBBBBBB, BBBBBBBB batman; CCCCCCCC, CCCCCCCC catman; DDDDDDDD, DDDDDDDD datman . . . ."

---

### Phonics Assessment

Use the Phonics Assessment (pages 227–230) to determine which letters each student can identify and which letter sounds each student can produce.

---

# Phonics Activities *(cont.)*

## Alphabet Book Project

Use the Student Alphabet Book Directions (pages 182–190) and the Alphabet Book Patterns (pages 218–226) to create individual student alphabet books featuring student artwork for each letter of the alphabet.

## Preparation

Copy a set of Alphabet Book Pages and Cover (pages 191–217) for each student. The students will be adding construction paper cutouts, yarn, and other items to each page. The book will become thick and should be bound using "o" rings or a commercial book binder. Coordinate the development of the book with your curriculum and complete each letter as it is studied throughout the year. The students will enjoy reviewing and learning from the pages they have already completed. The Alphabet Book Patterns (pages 218–226) may be substituted with die-cuts if they are available. Set aside each art project as it is completed, and allow each page to dry before closing and storing the book.

## Directions for Each Letter

A list of materials is included, giving the different materials needed to complete a letter project page for one student. Scissors, glue, and pencils are not typically included in the materials list. These materials should, however, be on hand for each project. Some of the steps may be completed by the teacher and others by the students, depending on the development level of the students. The preparation section for each letter explains what the teacher should do before the activity.

# Aa is for apple

**Materials:** apple pattern (page 218), construction paper (red, green, or yellow), crayons

**Preparation:** Copy the apple pattern onto construction paper.

**Directions:** Cut out the apple. Demonstrate how to "take a bite" out of the apple by gently tearing one side. Glue the apple to the page and draw a stem and leaf.

# Bb is for ball

**Materials:** triangle pattern (page 218), construction paper (orange, blue, yellow, green, red, and violet)

**Preparation:** Copy six triangle patterns onto construction paper (one of each color). Cut out the triangles.

**Directions:** Demonstrate how to arrange the triangles by placing the points together to form the shape of a ball. Glue the shapes to the page to form a ball.

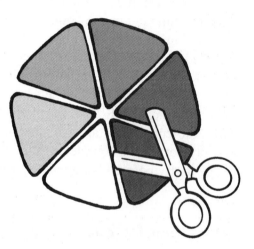

# Cc is for cookies

**Materials:** circle pattern (page 218), tan construction paper, brown construction paper (optional), assortment of crayons, markers, sequins, and stickers

**Preparation:** Copy three circle patterns onto construction paper.

**Directions:** Cut out the circles. Glue the circles to the page and decorate using crayons, markers, sequins, or stickers. (You may hole-punch brown construction paper to create chocolate chips, or glue colored confetti to make sprinkles.)

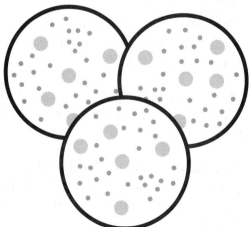

# Dd is for dinosaur

**Materials:** dinosaur head and body patterns (page 219), brad, construction paper

**Preparation:** Copy the dinosaur patterns onto construction paper. Cut out the dinosaur.

**Directions:** Demonstrate how to connect the dinosaur head to the body using a brad. Glue only the body to the page so the head may be moved freely.

# Ee is for elephant

**Materials:** elephant head and body patterns (page 220), gray or purple construction paper, brad, gray yarn

**Preparation:** Copy the elephant pattern onto construction paper. Cut out the elephant head. Cut the yarn into 1" pieces. Tie a knot at one end of each length of yarn.

**Directions:** Cut out the elephant body. Demonstrate how to connect the head to the body using a brad. Glue the elephant body to the page. Glue a piece of yarn to the body for the elephant's tail.

# Ff is for fish

**Materials:** fish pattern (page 221), white construction paper, aluminum foil, *The Rainbow Fish*, leftover pieces of construction paper

**Preparation:** Copy the fish pattern onto construction paper. Cut out a small fin from aluminum foil. Cut out the fish.

**Directions:** Create colored stripes and fins using leftover pieces of construction paper. Read aloud the story, *The Rainbow Fish*. Glue the aluminum foil fin to the fish. Glue the fish to the page.

# Gg is for gumballs

**Materials:** gumball machine pattern (page 221), white construction paper, round stickers or multicolored round foam circles.

**Preparation:** Copy the gumball machine pattern onto construction paper. Cut out the gumball machine.

**Directions:** Glue the gumball machine to the page. Attach 10 round stickers or glue 10 foam circles in the machine for gumballs.

# Hh is for house

**Materials:** house roof pattern (page 222), crayons, markers, brown or red construction paper

**Preparation:** Copy the house roof pattern onto construction paper. Cut out the roof. Cut out a square to create a house for the roof.

**Directions:** Demonstrate how to glue the triangle on top of the square to create a house. Show how to add windows, a chimney, a door, grass, sun, and clouds using crayons or markers. Glue the triangle and square on the page. Use crayons or markers to finish the house and background.

# Ii is for insects

**Materials:** black, red, and green water-based inkpads, black markers, construction paper

**Directions:** Demonstrate how to create fingerprint insects in a variety of sizes and colors. Show how to add two antennae, six legs, and two eyes to create examples of the insects seen outside. Make several fingerprint insects. On the red fingerprints, add black dots to create ladybugs.

# Jj is for jump rope

**Materials:** jump rope handles pattern (page 222), construction paper, thick string or yarn, tape

**Preparation:** Copy the jump rope patterns onto construction paper and cut them out. Measure and cut a 9" length of string for each student.

**Directions:** Tape the yarn to the handles and glue the handles to the page.

# Kk is for kite

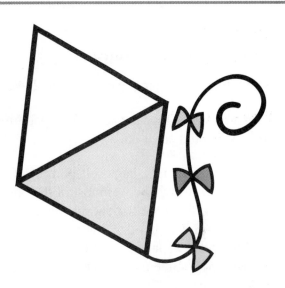

**Materials:** triangle pattern (page 218), two different colors of construction paper, markers or crayons

**Preparation:** Copy one triangle onto each color of construction paper and cut out the triangles.

**Directions:** Demonstrate how to place the pair of construction-paper triangles together to form a kite. Glue the triangles to the page. Draw a tail for the kite.

# Ll is for lion

**Materials:** lion head and mane patterns (page 222), yellow and tan construction paper, two wiggly eyes, tiny black pompom

**Preparation:** Copy the lion head pattern onto tan construction paper. Copy the lion mane pattern onto yellow construction paper. Cut out the mane and head.

**Directions:** Demonstrate how to place scissors on the cut lines and cut around the circumference of the mane and bend the cuts in opposite directions to create the appearance of a mane. Glue the mane on the page. Glue the head atop the mane. Glue wiggly eyes and a tiny black pom-pom for the nose. Draw the lion's mouth and whiskers.

# Mm is for mittens

**Materials:** mitten patterns (page 223), construction paper, string or yarn, tape, assortment of ribbons, sequins, glitter glue, crayons, and markers

**Preparation:** Copy the mitten patterns onto construction paper. Cut a 4" length of string.

**Directions:** Cut out the mittens. Tape the yarn to the back of each mitten. Glue the mittens to the page. Use ribbons, sequins, glitter glue, crayons, and markers to decorate each mitten and create a matching pair.

# Nn is for newspaper

**Materials:** newspaper pattern (page 224), newspaper

**Preparation:** Trace the newspaper pattern onto newspaper and cut it out.

**Directions:** Draw a large self-portrait. Demonstrate how to make the drawing cover most of the blank space on the page. Show how the student may place the newspaper cutout over his or her drawing to appear that he or she is reading the newspaper. (The head should be above the dashed line.) Glue newspaper cutout to the page.

# Oo is for octopus

**Materials:** finger paint, paintbrushes, two wiggly eyes

**Directions:** Paint the student's hand with his or her choice of color combinations. Place the handprint on the page with fingers pointing toward the letter Oo and palms located near the top of the page. Paint the other hand and have the student overlap the handprint with his or her fingers pointing in the opposite direction in order to make eight tentacles. (The base of the hand creates the body of the octopus. The fingers make the tentacles.) Allow to dry overnight. Add wiggly eyes. Draw a mouth on the octopus.

# Pp is for pizza

**Materials:** pizza crust and pepperoni patterns (page 224), circle pattern (page 218), tan, dark red, and light red construction paper, white yarn

**Preparation:** Copy the pizza crust pattern onto tan construction paper. Copy three pepperoni patterns onto dark red construction paper. Copy the circle pattern (pizza sauce) onto light red construction paper. Cut half-inch strips of white yarn.

**Directions:** Glue the pizza crust to the page. Glue the pizza sauce on top of the crust. Apply glue in a zigzag pattern on top of the sauce. Add the yarn "cheese" and the pepperoni to the pizza.

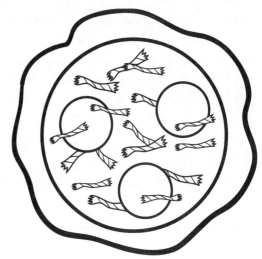

# Qq is for quilt

**Materials:** quilt pattern (page 223), two colors of construction paper, white construction paper

**Preparation:** Copy the quilt pattern onto white construction paper and cut it out. Cut nine 1" squares from two different colors of construction paper.

**Directions:** Demonstrate how to use the two colors to create an AB pattern. Glue the quilt on the page. Glue the squares onto the quilt to create a patchwork pattern. Assist the students in gluing the squares inside the quilt pattern if necessary.

# Rr is for rainbow

**Materials:** crayons (red, orange, yellow, green, blue, indigo, violet)

**Directions:** Find each of the following crayons: red, orange, yellow, green, blue, indigo, and violet. Create a rainbow by drawing a half circle. Use the colors in the above order to create a rainbow on the page.

---

# Ss is for sun

**Materials:** finger paint (red, yellow, orange), black crayon

**Directions:** Use the finger paint to create your own sun on the page. Allow to dry overnight. Add eyes and a mouth using a black crayon.

---

# Tt is for toothbrush

**Materials:** toothbrush handle and toothpaste patterns (page 225), light blue and another color of construction paper, tissue paper, stapler

**Preparation:** Copy the toothbrush handle pattern onto construction paper. Cut out the handle. Copy the toothpaste pattern onto light blue construction paper and cut it out. Fold several layers of tissue paper into a 2" rectangle and staple on one side to hold together. Fold the toothbrush handle in half and staple the tissue-paper rectangle at the top of the toothbrush handle.

**Directions:** Demonstrate how to use scissors to make ½" cuts across the exposed tissue-paper rectangle to create toothbrush bristles. Glue the toothbrush to the page. Then glue the toothpaste on top of the toothbrush.

# Uu is for umbrella

**Materials:** umbrella pattern (page 225), construction paper, markers

**Preparation:** Copy the umbrella pattern onto construction paper. Cut out the umbrella.

**Directions:** Glue the umbrella to the page. Use markers to draw an umbrella handle and rain drops.

# Vv is for vine

**Materials:** green construction paper, green crayon

**Preparation:** Cut out five small hearts from green construction paper.

**Directions:** Demonstrate how a vine appears to be a series of squiggly lines. Draw a series of squiggly lines on the page. Glue the hearts to the lines to create a vine. Draw additional hearts on the lines.

# Ww is for windmill

**Materials:** triangle pattern (page 218), construction paper

**Preparation:** Copy four triangles onto construction paper and cut them out. Cut out a 2" x 1" rectangle from construction paper.

**Directions:** Glue the rectangle vertically on the bottom of the page. Arrange and glue the triangles with the points toward the top center of the rectangle to create a windmill.

# Xx is for x-ray

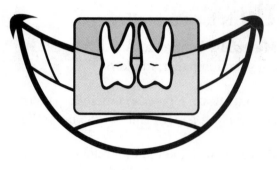

**Materials:** open-mouth pattern (page 226), old dental x-rays (from a dentist)

**Preparation:** Cut out teeth from the x-rays. Cut out the mouth.

**Directions:** Glue the mouth on the page. Glue the x-ray section on top of the teeth, inside the mouth.

# Yy is for yo-yo

**Materials:** circle pattern (page 218), construction paper, ribbon or yarn, tape

**Preparation:** Copy two circles onto construction paper. Cut a 7" length of ribbon and create a loop at one end.

**Directions:** Cut out the circles. Glue one circle to the bottom of the page. Tape the straight end of the ribbon to the middle of the circle. Glue the other circle on top of the ribbon to create a yo-yo. Give the loop of string to the page.

# Zz is for zebra

**Materials:** zebra body and zebra tail patterns (page 226), white construction paper, black crayon, wiggly eye, brad

**Preparation:** Copy the zebra pattern onto construction paper. Cut out the zebra body and tail.

**Directions:** Use a black crayon to add stripes to the zebra. Glue a wiggly eye on the zebra. Use a brad to attach the zebra's tail. Glue only the zebra body to the page.

# My Alphabet Book

By _____

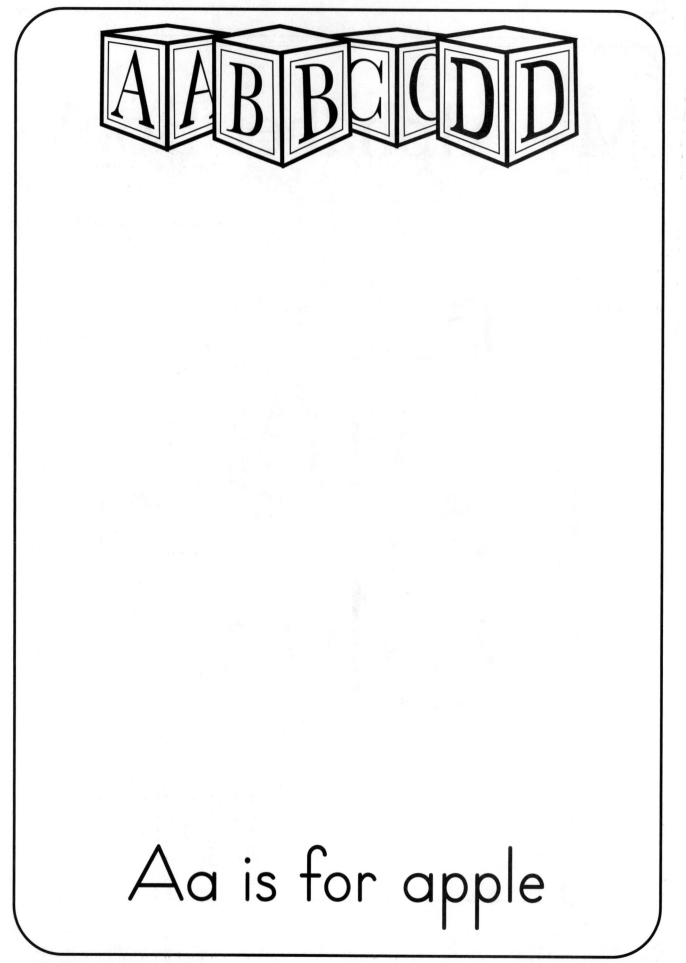

Aa is for apple

Bb is for ball

Cc is for cookies

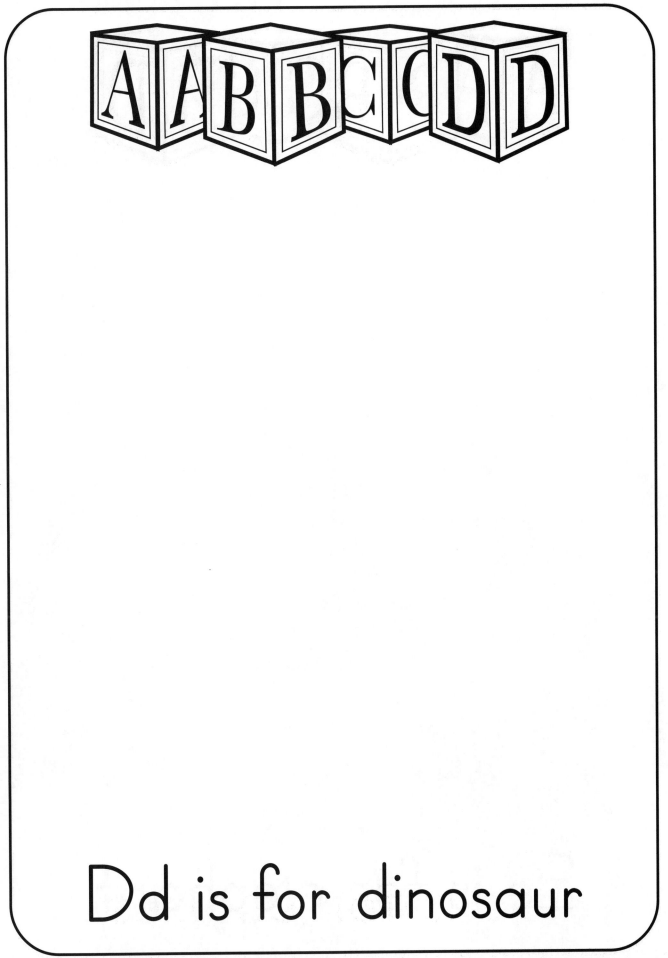

# Dd is for dinosaur

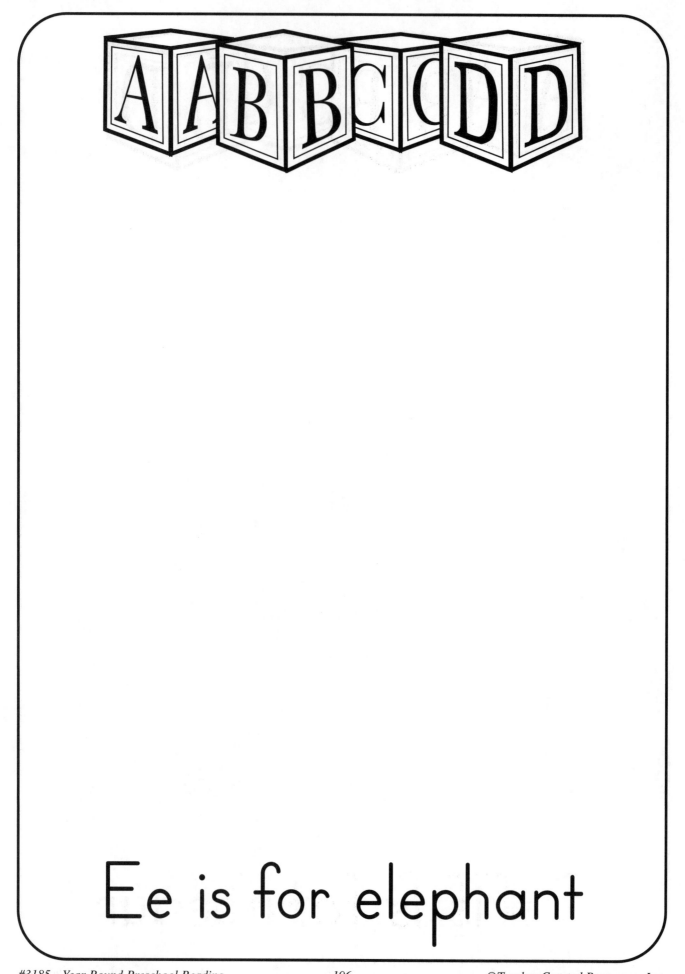

Ee is for elephant

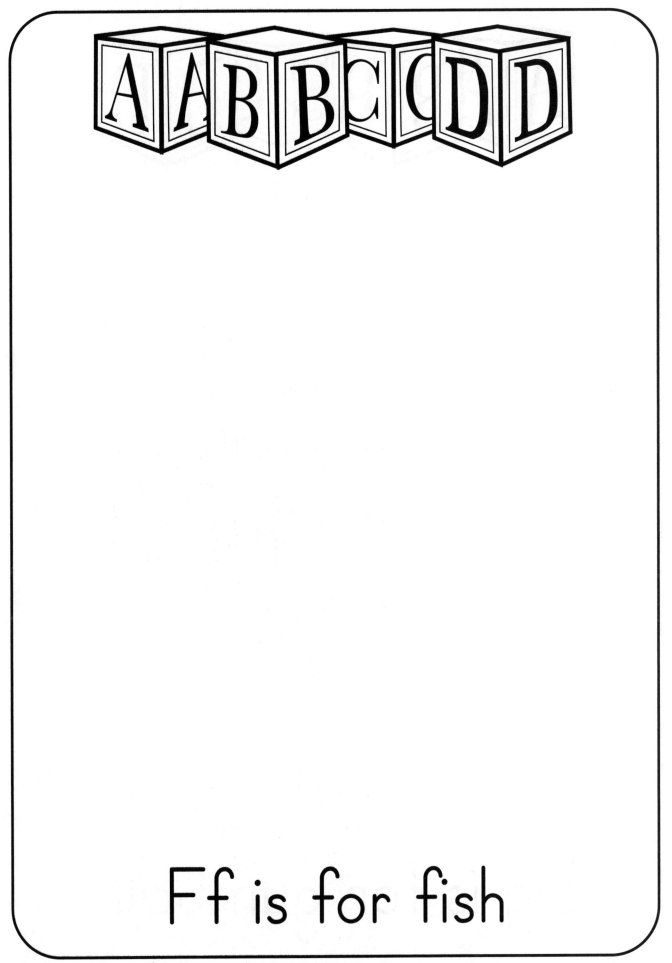

Ff is for fish

Gg is for gumballs

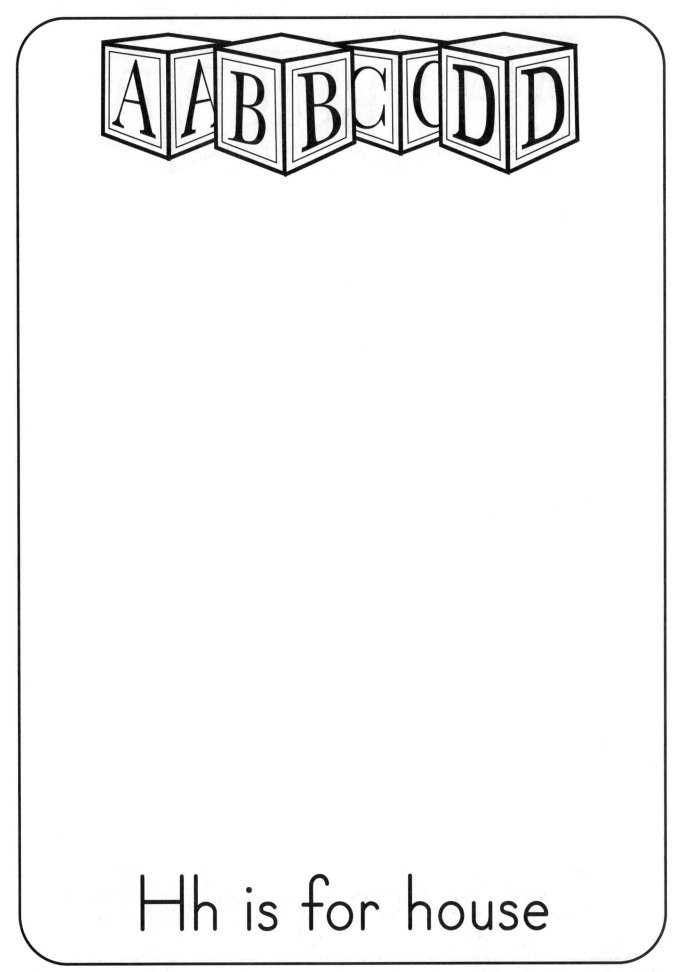

Hh is for house

Ii is for insects

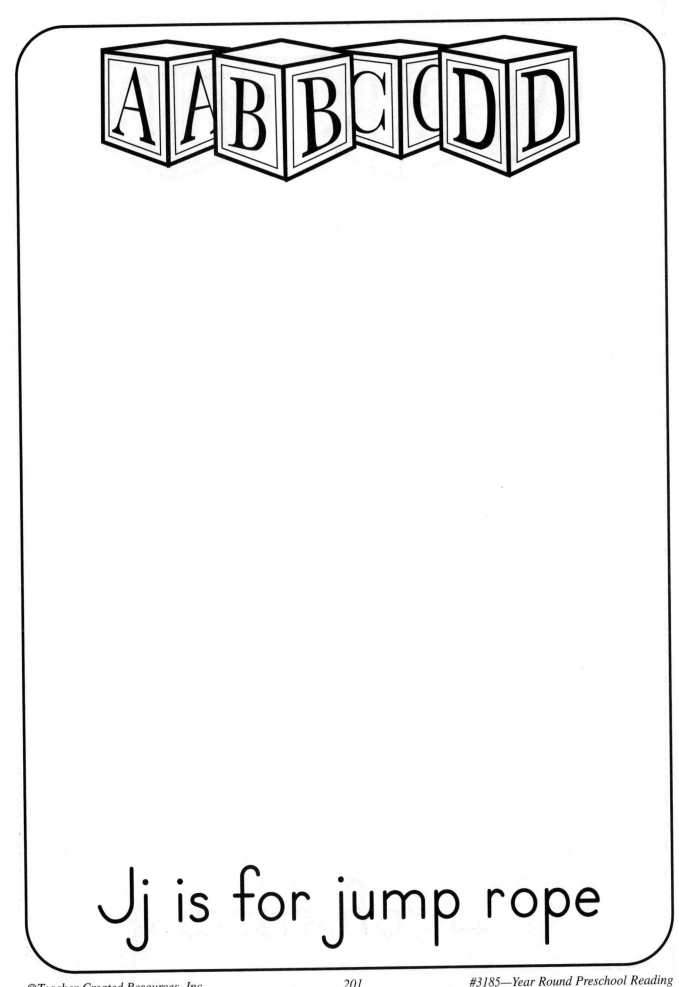

Jj is for jump rope

Kk is for kite

Ll is for lion

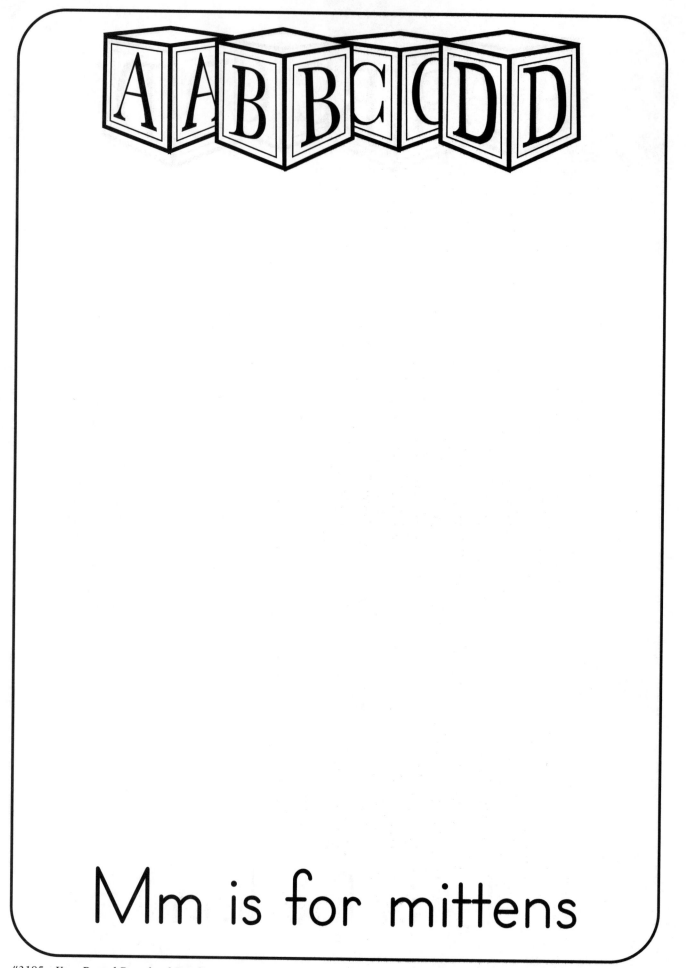

# Mm is for mittens

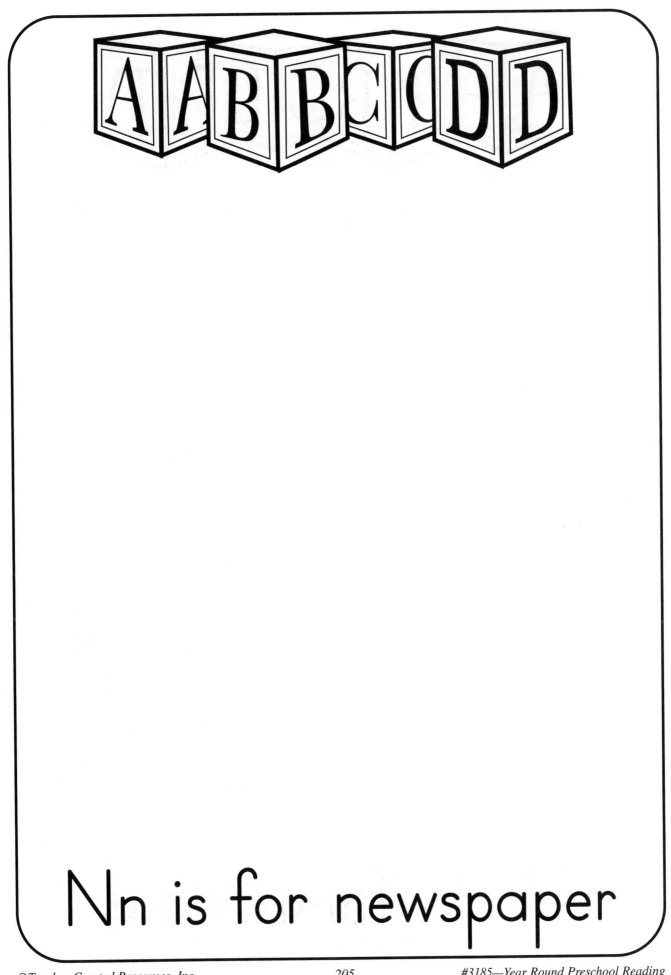

Nn is for newspaper

Oo is for octopus

Pp is for pizza

Qq is for quilt

Rr is for rainbow

Ss is for sun

Tt is for toothbrush

Uu is for umbrella

Vv is for vine

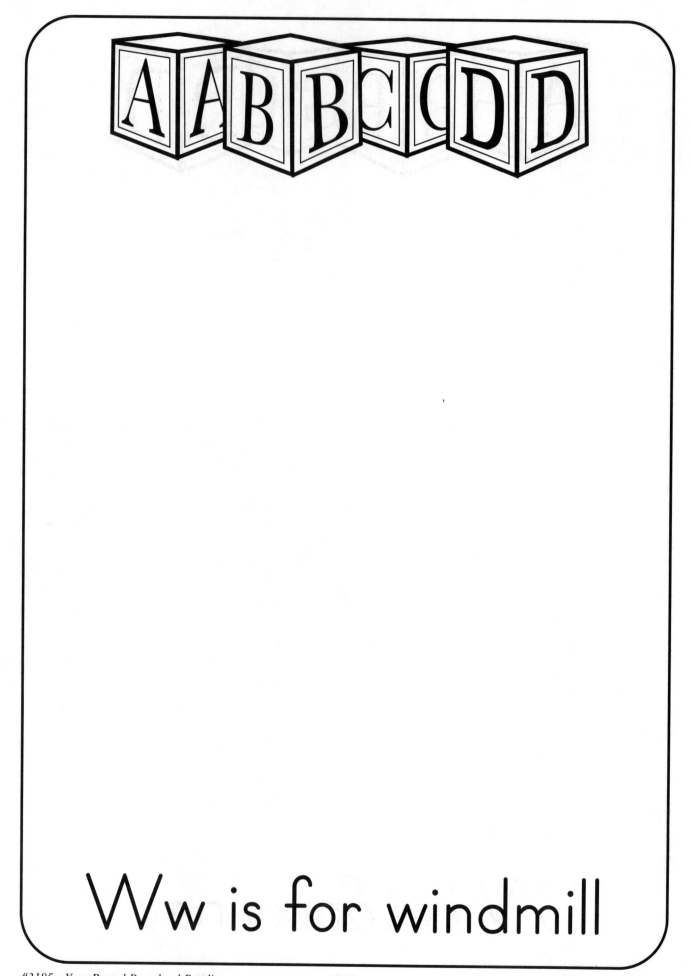

Ww is for windmill

Xx is for x-ray

Yy is for yo-yo

# Zz is for zebra

**apple**

**cookie,
yo-yo,
and pizza**

**ball,
kite,
and
windmill**

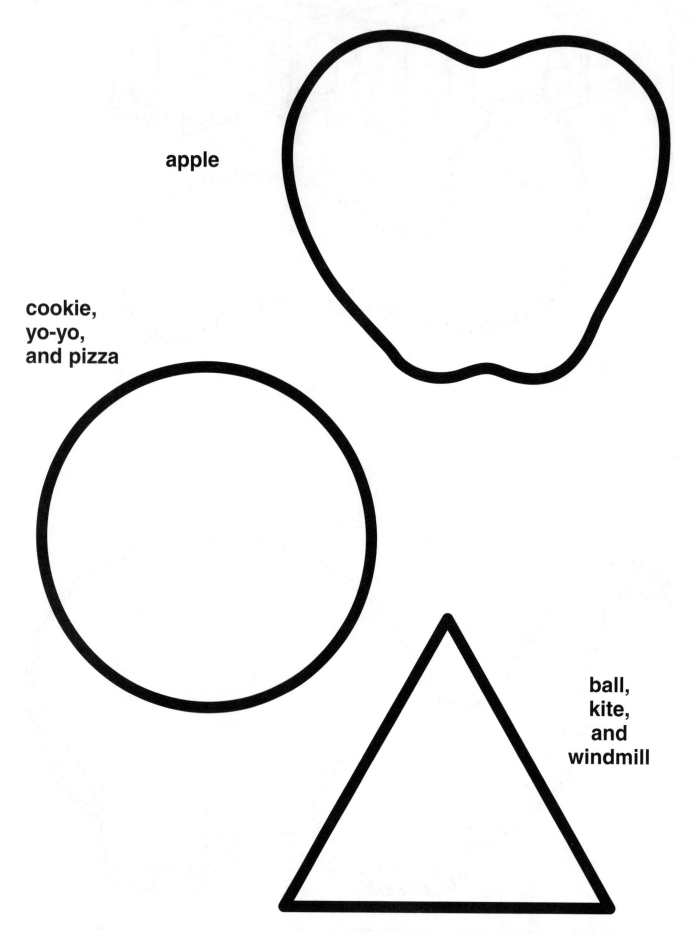

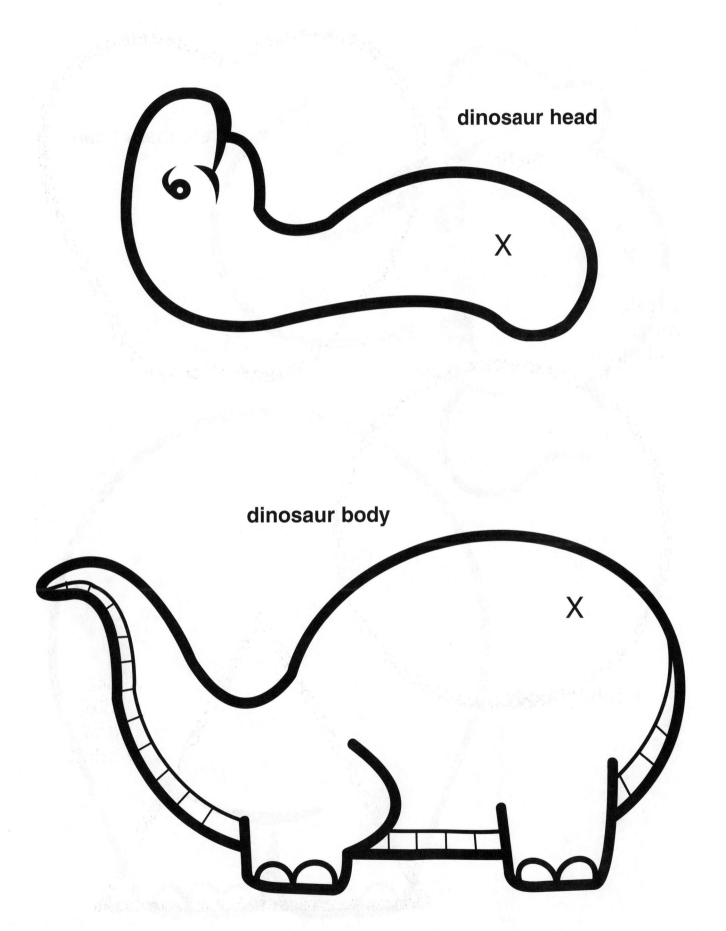

**dinosaur head**

X

**dinosaur body**

X

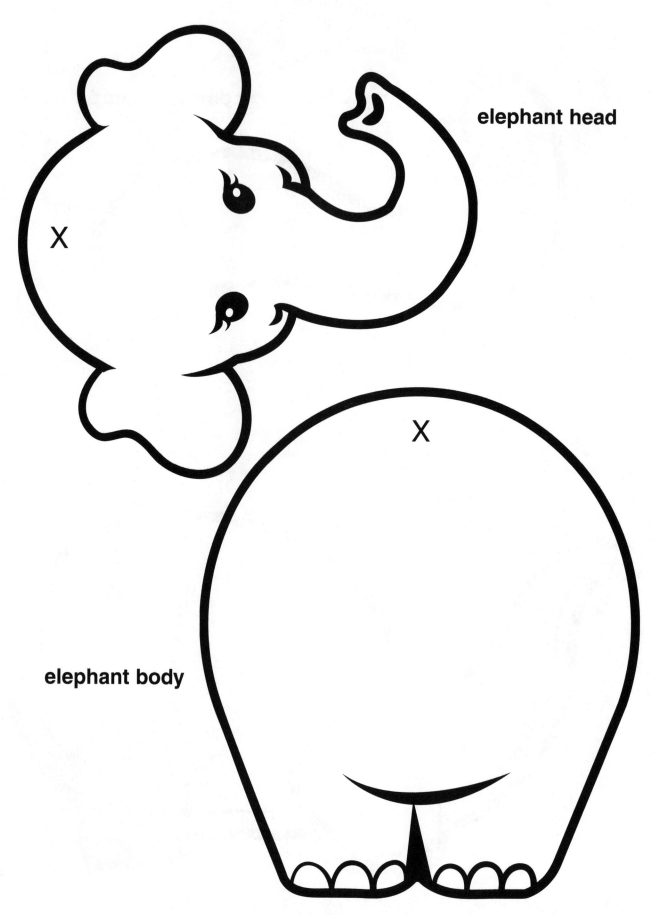

elephant head

X

X

elephant body

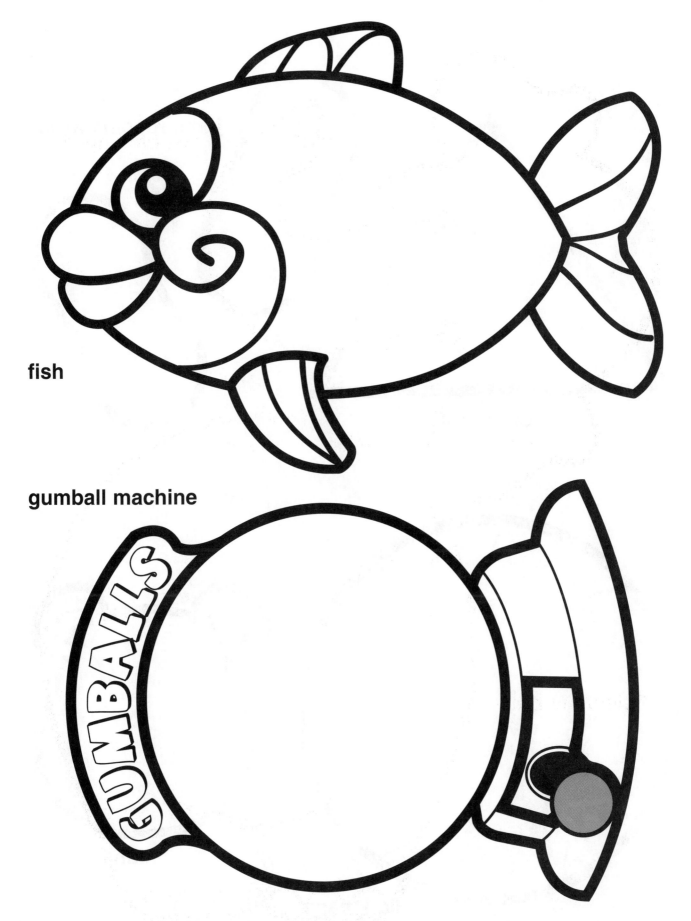

**fish**

**gumball machine**

**jump rope handles**

**house roof**

**lion mane**

**lion head**

**mittens**

**quilt**

**newspaper**

**pepperoni**

**pizza crust**

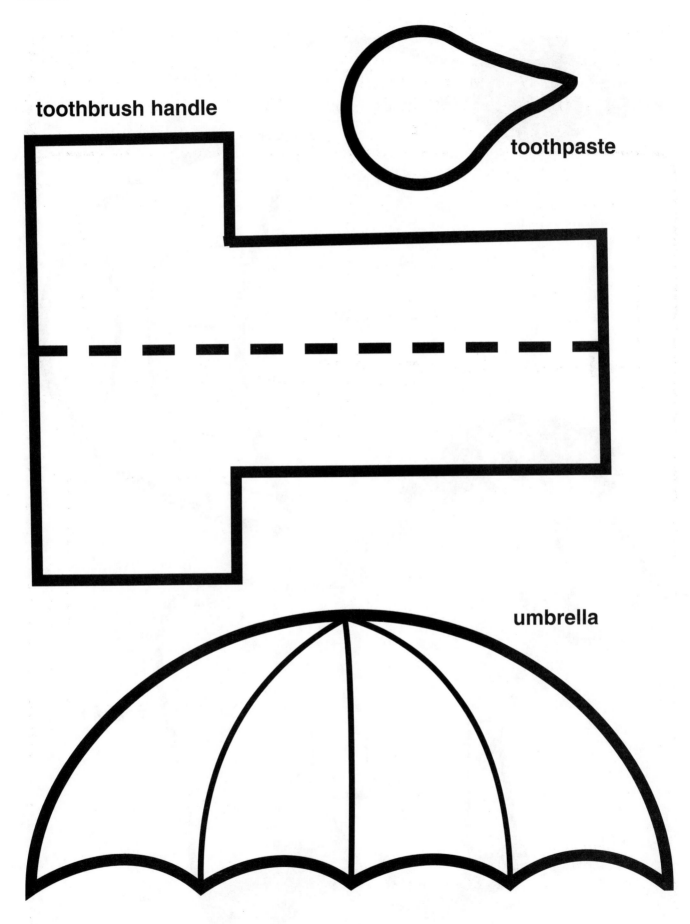

**toothbrush handle**

**toothpaste**

**umbrella**

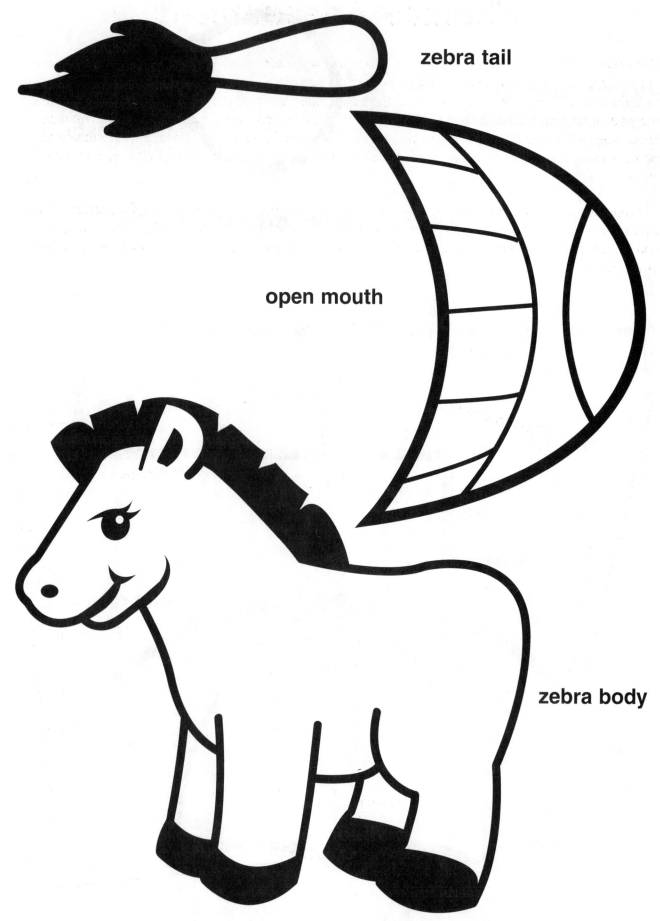

zebra tail

open mouth

zebra body

# Phonics Assessment

**Directions:** Make one copy of pages 229–230 to use with each student during assessment. Make one copy of page 228 for each student. Begin with the uppercase letters. Show the student page 229, the uppercase letters, one row at a time. Note that some letters are repeated in different fonts. First, ask the student to name each uppercase letter. Mark an X in the corresponding box on the student data sheet (page 228) to indicate the letters the student has correctly identified. Then, ask the student to produce the corresponding sound. Again, mark an X in the corresponding box on the student data sheet.

Continue the assessment by showing the student the copy of page 230, for the lowercase letters. Once again, mark an X in the corresponding box on the student data sheet to indicate the lowercase letters and sounds the student has correctly identified. Use the student data sheet to determine which lessons you will use.

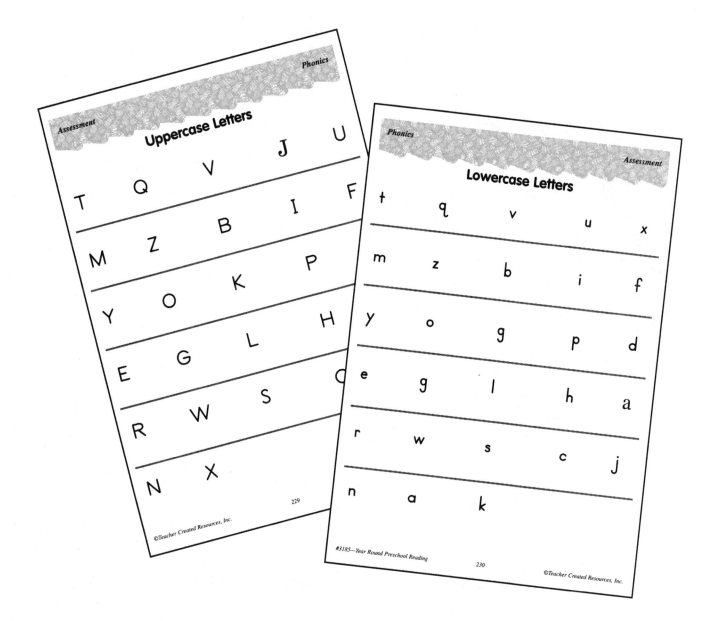

# Student Data Sheet

Student's Name _____    Date _____

| Uppercase Letters | Identifies Letter | Produces Sound |
|---|---|---|
| T | | |
| Q | | |
| V | | |
| J | | |
| U | | |
| M | | |
| Z | | |
| B | | |
| I | | |
| F | | |
| Y | | |
| O | | |
| K | | |
| P | | |
| D | | |
| E | | |
| G | | |
| L | | |
| H | | |
| A | | |
| R | | |
| W | | |
| S | | |
| C | | |
| J | | |
| N | | |
| X | | |
| Totals | ____/27 | ____/27 |

| Lowercase Letters | Identifies Letter | Produces Sound |
|---|---|---|
| t | | |
| q | | |
| v | | |
| u | | |
| x | | |
| m | | |
| z | | |
| b | | |
| i | | |
| f | | |
| y | | |
| o | | |
| g | | |
| p | | |
| d | | |
| e | | |
| g | | |
| l | | |
| h | | |
| a | | |
| r | | |
| w | | |
| s | | |
| c | | |
| j | | |
| n | | |
| a | | |
| k | | |
| Totals | ____/28 | ____/28 |

# Uppercase Letters

| | | | | |
|---|---|---|---|---|
| T | Q | V | **J** | U |

| | | | | |
|---|---|---|---|---|
| M | Z | B | I | F |

| | | | | |
|---|---|---|---|---|
| Y | O | K | P | D |

| | | | | |
|---|---|---|---|---|
| E | G | L | H | A |

| | | | | |
|---|---|---|---|---|
| R | W | S | C | J |

| | |
|---|---|
| N | X |

# Lowercase Letters

t      q      v      u      x

---

m      z      b      i      f

---

y      o      g      p      d

---

e      **g**      l      h      **a**

---

r      w      s      c      j

---

n      a      k

# Fine Motor Skills Activities

*Fine motor skills* involve small muscle movements—those that occur in the fingers in coordination with the eyes. Preschoolers develop their fine motor skills through hands-on activities designed to strengthen the hand, wrist, arm, and shoulder muscles. The following activities focus on enhancing the finger and hand muscles necessary for writing and future letter formation.

## Tracing Activities

1. Copy the Pencil Grip Page (page 232). Discuss pencil grip with students.

2. Reproduce the Tracing Practice Pages (pages 234-236). Allow your students to practice drawing the circle, triangle, and square shapes. Introduce one line shape at a time. Have the students practice the line shape two or more times before introducing a new shape. As the students learn to draw the different line shapes, introduce art activities that coordinate with your curriculum and each shape. For example, draw a circle-shaped pumpkin to paint while studying the fall season.

3. Coordinate your tracing activities with the study of different alphabet letters. Practice drawing vertical, horizontal, and half-circle lines during lessons on forming the uppercase and lowercase letters *Ll, Tt, Hh, Ii,* and *Ff*. Practice drawing right and left curved lines during lessons on forming the uppercase and lowercase letters *Dd, Pp, Bb, Rr, Jj,* and *Uu*. Practice drawing left and right diagonal lines during the lessons on forming the uppercase and lowercase letters *Xx, Yy, Nn, Zz, Aa, Kk, Mm, Ww,* and *Vv*. Practice drawing wavy lines during lessons on forming uppercase and lowercase *Ss, Cc,* and *Gg*. Practice drawing circular lines during lessons on the uppercase and lowercase *Oo* and *Qq*.

## Cutting Activities

1. Copy the Using Scissors Page (page 233) and discuss proper use of scissors.

2. Copy the Cutting Practice Pages (pages 237-238) and allow your students to practice cutting each line shape. Introduce only one line shape at a time. Repeat cutting out each shape multiple times before introducing a new shape. Coordinate cutting activities with curriculum and art activities.

3. Coordinate cutting activities with the study of different alphabet letters using the format outlined above in Tracing Activities #3.

## Fine Motor Skills Assessment

An assessment is included for Fine Motor Skills on pages 239–240. Copy the pages and ask the students to trace each shape with their finger, then with a pencil or crayon. Then, ask the students to follow the lines and cut out each individual shape.

# Pencil Grip

A correct pencil grip will help a student in everything from drawing basic shapes to printing, to handwriting. Introducing a correct pencil grip to your students by demonstrating it may be the only instruction some students will need; however, many students need repeated practice and demonstrations of an acceptable position for the fingers when holding and using a pencil (or other writing tool).

## Pencil Grip

An acceptable pencil grip is any grip on the pencil in which a circle is formed by the thumb and index finger, once the fingers are holding the pencil. After the fingers have been placed on the pencil, they should be able to freely move the pencil. Typically, the thumb and index finger are opposite each other. The thumb is on the bottom and the index finger is on the top of the pencil. The middle finger usually supports the pencil while the ring finger and the little finger are bent and resting in the palm. However, there are other positions for the middle finger, ring finger, and little finger that will still yield an acceptable pencil grip.

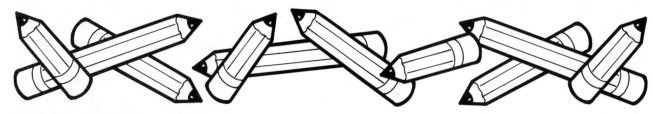

# Using Scissors .

The idea of controlling an object to make cuts is a fascinating one. You usually will not have a difficult time persuading children to use scissors. Children undoubtedly will have seen adults using scissors and often have a desire to learn how to use them.

When introducing scissors, remember to discuss safety with the children. Remind them that children only use scissors for cutting objects when an adult gives them permission. You may also want to give some directions about properly and safely handling scissors.

In addition, you will want to provide some instruction regarding correct ways of holding scissors. Determine a student's hand dominance, if appropriate. The student's thumb will go in one hole and, for many, the pointer and middle finger will go in the other hole. The ring and little finger should be bent in the palm for stability. (If a student has a difficult time keeping fingers bent, have him or her hold an eraser or wadded-up piece of paper in the ring and little finger while holding the scissors.)

When cutting, the thumb should be pointed up toward the ceiling. The elbow and arm (of the hand holding the scissors) should be held in toward the body. The hand holding the paper is the same hand (and arm) that moves and rotates the paper.

Scissors activities are provided on the following pages. The activities are listed in sequential order, following a progression of cutting skills.

**Teacher Note:** Have plenty of supervision if you are introducing scissors for the first time to a large group of children. It is preferable to do this in small groups. Be sure to provide plenty of time for children to experiment with the scissors the first time they are allowed to handle them.

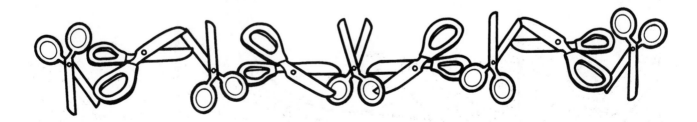

# Tracing Practice

**Directions:** Practice tracing along the dotted lines.

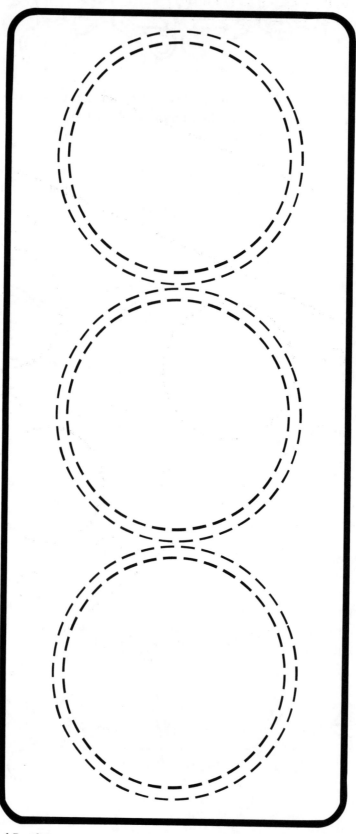

# Tracing Practice *(cont.)*

**Directions:** Practice tracing along the dotted lines.

# Tracing Practice (cont.)

**Directions:** Practice tracing along the dotted lines.

236

# Cutting Practice

**Directions:** Practice cutting along each line.

# Cutting Practice *(cont.)*

## Sammy Snake

**Directions:** Color Sammy Snake. Cut out Sammy Snake. Make Sammy Snake by cutting on the dotted line. Begin at the star on the tail. For fun, tie a string on the end of your snake, so that you can hang it up.

# Fine Motor Skills Assessment

**Directions:** Complete each shape by drawing the second half to match the first half. Connect the dotted lines on the first shape to see how it's done. Cut out the shapes.

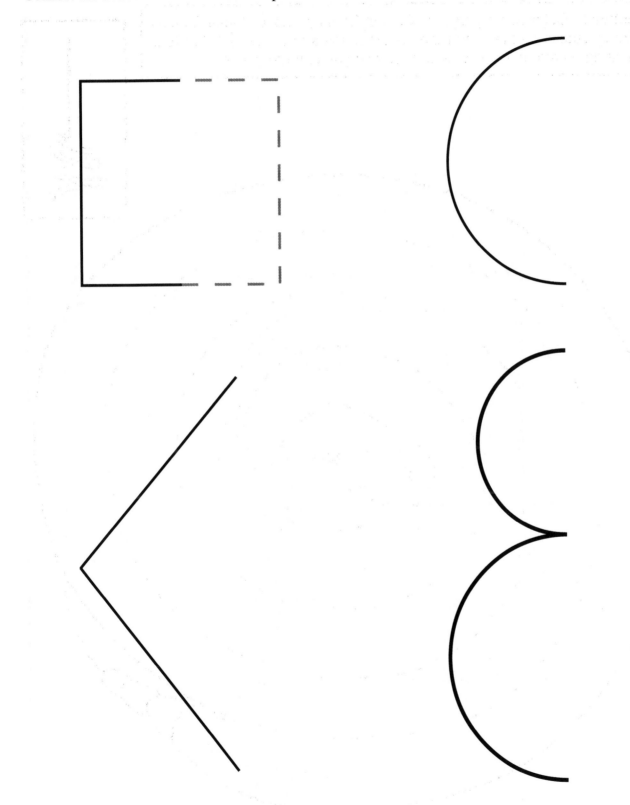

# Fine Motor Skills Assessment

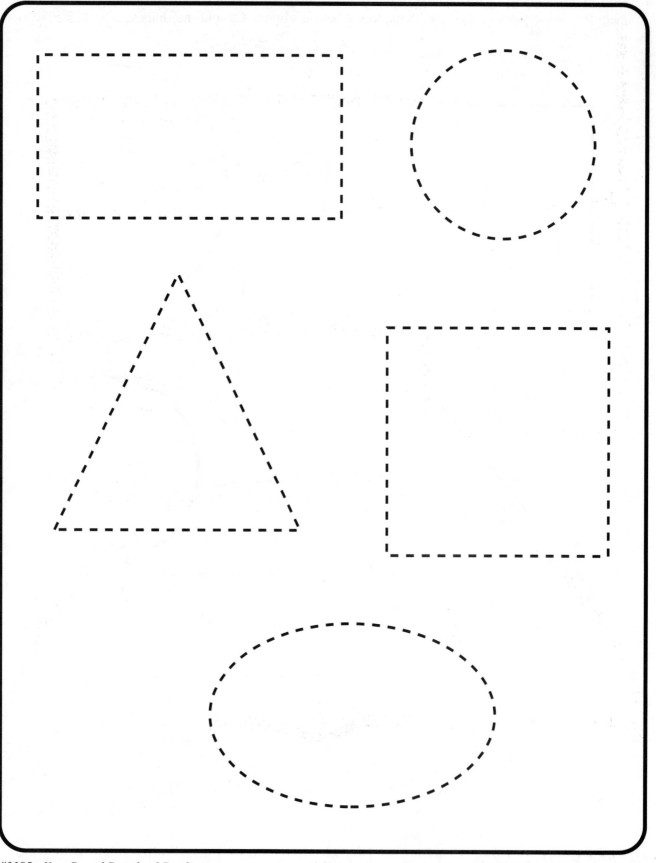